Outstanding Women
Living Extraordinary Lives

How women can overcome
A traumatic past
And move on to a successful future

By Tori Vigil

Author of Surviving the Teenage Journey

The women's testimonies and stories in this book are true and used by permission; however some names may have been left out to protect identities.

The philanthropic organizations listed in this book are all in good standing at the time of publication, however websites often change, and some websites listed may no longer be available to the reader.

Contact the Author via her website

http://torivigil.tripod.com

-BOOKER T. WASHINGTON-

"I have learned that success is to be measured

Not so much by the position that one has reached in life

As by the obstacles overcome while trying to succeed."

-BESSIE STANLEY-

"Success is to laugh often and much;

To win the respect of intelligent people and the affection of children;

To earn the appreciation of honest critics

and endure the betrayal of false friends;

To appreciate beauty, to find the best in others;

To leave the world a bit better, whether by a healthy child, a garden patch

or a redeemed social condition;

To know even one life has breathed easier because you have lived.

This is to have succeeded."

My prayer for you

Dear Heavenly Father,

Bless the woman reading this today. Help her to see she is beautiful inside, and out. Abundantly bless her life in every area. Reveal to her your hidden truths Lord. May she walk in her destiny, and live her life with purpose. Father, light her path with your loving guidance; and show her that we are never alone, that it is you who carry us through life's rough patches.

In Jesus name I pray.

Amen

TABLE OF CONTENTS:

Acknowledgements

Using only written words to say thank you to the many women in my life: my friends, my sisters, my daughters, and other family, coworkers, employers, and employees who have helped me become a better person seems insufficient. I'm not sure I can express my gratitude for all that they have done to better my life in many ways. They have prayed with me, listened to me, encouraged me, believed in me, and let me cry on their shoulder. I hope they all know how truly thankful I am for all that they helped do to contribute to my life, this book, and in turn to the lives of the readers.

This book is dedicated to

My Mother Rita, and My Grandmother Luisita.

The two of you are the outstanding and virtuous women in my life; whom thanks to your encouragement, guidance and powerful prayers have helped me become the woman I am today. Like many other women who have dedicated themselves to their children your resume may not be long and worthy of a notation in Who's Who in life, but you carry with you a resume of the heart. Your deeds may be unsung in this world, but their effects are long lasting. Your words of wisdom are not well known, but their power touches the souls of those who hear them. Your teachings may not grace the pages of history books, but the lessons learned from them will be passed on to future generations. Mothers are often the unsung, and unseen hero's behind the lives of many great men, and women. I'm not sure I can say anything that would be sufficient enough to express what you mean to me so I will simply say thank you, and I love you.

I also wish to thank the wonderful ladies from the Outstanding Women in America Organization for sharing their lives, and their stories with me and my readers; their faith in God, in themselves, and in me have made this book possible. I look forward to meeting all the new members that will come into this organization in the future. I know they will be just as blessed, and as much of a blessing as the women in this book.

A special thanks to my sisters for believing in me, to my daughters for encouraging me, Ray for your help in formatting this book, and to my friends Cecilia, Jessica, and Traci; your anticipation to read this book has kept me on track with my writing so I could get this done.

Please feel free to write in this book, I've always thought that the best of books are worth making notes in, and a tattered book means that it is well used. There are note pages at the end of each chapter to make it easy for you to write down your thoughts.

Introduction

"Lord let me be an instrument of your peace.

Where there is hatred, let me sow love;

where there is injury, pardon;

where there is doubt, faith;

where there is despair, hope;

where there is darkness, light"...

-Saint Francis of Assisi-

Are you ready to be taken on a great adventure, on a wonderful journey of womanhood? Join me as we travel into the lives of some seemingly ordinary women, just like you, whom after overcoming traumas from their past, now lead extraordinary lives. These women of faith have proudly proclaimed that they are followers of Jesus Christ, whom through his life and teachings lifted women to higher levels of dignity and respect. Though the faith of these women has been nurtured in different churches, and denominations they are all one in Christ, and share a love for humanity; and a deep passion for helping other women.

Isn't it funny how we often want to share our story with others, but don't know how, sometimes we just think that no one would be interested in our story so there would be no point in sharing it anyway? When I heard the stories of these women it resonated with my own story. We had all gone through some kind of trauma in our past, and had to turn to God, and leaned on him to get us through it. I heard each one of these women say they wanted to share their story, and like them, I also knew their stories needed to be told. So, I set about to write this book and share our stories with you, the reader. What I've learned in writing this book is that as I've written my story, and their stories it is no longer just my story, or just their story. It is a story, a moment from the past that no longer exists, but that we can all learn from. Writing has helped me to let go of my identification with the past.

You see life has a wondrous way of teaching us our greatest lessons, growing our wisdom, and strengthening our faith; but for many people that often happens after hardship, pain, sacrifice, prayer, and an act of faith. I'm sure you've heard the old saying, "what doesn't kill you makes you stronger". That couldn't be more true than for the women you are about to meet. These women opted to believe that every storm that came into their lives was so God could build their faith, perfect their character, and prepare them for the future; and the same can be true for you.

I am not my past; I am not just my story. These women are not their past, they are not just their story, and neither are you. I am, they are, and you are spiritual beings with unlimited potential, and we all have a divine connection with our Creator. I share our stories with you to show you what we've learned from the past, and how that drew us closer to God.

Psalm 102:18 (GNT)

Write down for the coming generation

What the Lord has done,

So that people not yet born will praise him.

The women you are about to meet in this book are all professionals in their chosen fields, and members of the Outstanding Women in America National Honor Society. The National Honor Society is designed especially to empower lifetime recognition, for Christian women. The organization proudly pays tribute to their members Credentials by awarding National and

World Titles to these deserving women for the success they have been blessed with in their lives! As I interviewed, spent time with them, and got to know them I found my own faith growing. I laughed, and I cried as I heard about the miracles God has done in their lives. As these women overcame their traumatic pasts they also found hope for a bright future, as well as a desire to help others who have been through similar situations. It is my hope that I tell their stories well, and that your faith also grows after reading about how amazing God really is.

I know with all my heart that every woman has a story to tell interesting, unique, and like no one else's; an amazing story of strength and perseverance, of hope, and doubt, of good times and of struggles. Some stories are easy to tell, and others bare secrets we would much rather forget. Yet it is in telling our stories that we free ourselves from the hold those secrets can have on us, telling our stories can heal us and can help others too. There is a strength that can be found when women unite for a greater purpose. Every woman needs advice from time to time, and has advice to give as well. We could all use a little help finding out who we are, what we're here for, how to make better choices, and what it is we we're meant to do.

How much easier would life be for all women if every woman shared her story, her wisdom, and her knowledge with others? Imagine if no one was afraid to say I made a mistake, and this is how you can avoid making the same one. If we had the courage to tell others where it is we came from and what it was we had to overcome. It would be like a wild fire in a dry forest. It would spread from woman to woman growing in power and in brightness, lighting our way through a world of chaos and con-fusion. Truths that are passed from one woman to another, from one generation to the next; truths about finding true love, passion, faith, motherhood, and learning to trust ourselves.

(The previous two paragraphs were taken from

"Surviving the Teenage

Journey", another book by Tori Vigil)

I have been a writer ever since I learned how to write, my mother has poems I wrote for her, and short stories I used to write to regale my younger sisters with at bedtime. As I moved into my adult years, I started keeping a journal for every year, I then started writing for magazines and newspapers. As I was looking back at the things I had written in the past, I noticed a pattern: I write what I know, I write what I feel, I write to reflect on the things that have happened in my life. I write to promote my spiritual growth, I write to help others, and I write to heal. The process of writing something down, at least for me, is freeing; it lets out any negative energy, and allows me to see the situations in my life from a new perspective. If you learn from your writing, it also expands positive energy and promotes spiritual growth. I would have to say that my experiences with writing are very spiritual. It's as if I step out of my problems, and hand everything over to God by writing things down. In doing so, I think that for a brief moment, God grants me the gift of seeing the words on the page through his eyes. From that divine perspective I've been able to take action; change what wasn't working, appreciate what is working, be thankful for what I have been given, and wait in hopeful anticipation for the things I want and need.

I've found that not only does writing help to heal myself, but it can and has helped others who have read what I have written; that is why I wrote this book. It's my hope that in reading about my life, and the lives of these outstanding women you will be inspired to find, and pursue your own God given destiny. To overcome, and learn from what ever you may have experienced as a child, or young adult. My vision in life is to leave behind a legacy that will inspire women of all ages to live creatively, define their own womanhood, and embrace their destiny. Creative, smart, bold, and strong women help to build a thriving community, and a better world. By pursuing your destiny you'll have daily purpose, and a life lived with purpose is destined to be a successful one. There is no greater motivation than to love what you do, and do it because you love it; regardless of pay, status, or titles. Living with purpose makes getting up each morning a delight instead of a chore, as you look forward to the day and what God might bring to you at any moment.

NOTE:

The Outstanding Women in America members are inducted into the O.W.A National Honor Society and are presented with the rewards commemorating outstanding success for a lifetime of achievement. Candidates are inducted into the honor society based on the personal and professional achievements in their life in the Following (10) categories;

(1). <u>Marriage and Family Commitments</u>

(2). <u>Short Stories/Personal Testimonies</u>

(3). <u>Charity/Community Service</u>

(4.) <u>Pageant Titles/Judging /Production</u>

(5.) <u>Degrees Earned</u>

(6.) <u>Career Achievements</u>

(7.) <u>Personal Challenges</u>

(8.) <u>Leadership/Business</u>

(9.) <u>Honors, Awards, Publications</u>

(10.) <u>Talents/Gifts/Abilities</u>

Personal Notes

_____

_____

_____

_____

_____

_____

_____

_____

_____

_____

_____

_____

Chapter One

Outstanding Women

Proverbs 12:4

A virtuous woman is a crown...

What is an Outstanding Woman?

What comes to your mind when you think of an Outstanding Woman? Do you think of someone famous? Do you think of someone from the past that left their mark in history? Perhaps you think of the magazines that list 20 women who they think are outstanding, among them are usually lawyers, doctors, actresses, writers, and so on. Among those 20 women one of them is usually named woman of the year. Of course women like that are outstanding, but what about the mom who stayed by her child's bed all night keeping watch over her; The nurse that stood vigil next to her patient in his last hours of life; The grandmother who kneels by her bed every night to pray for her family; the wife who kisses her husband every morning before he goes to work where he will risk his life as a firefighter; or the daughter that prays for her father, a soldier, that he will come home safely from war?

Regardless of age, or race, these amazing unsung hero's quietly stepped up to do their small part to make the world better. I believe with all my heart that we are all connected to each other. Every act of love, joy, and kindness done no matter how small, or seemingly insignificant it may seem; adds more love, joy, and kindness to all mankind. These outstanding women are not faceless people. They are like you and me, and the women in your family. Each woman simply doing her best living everyday lives, but it is the small ordinary, everyday things that make the world what it is.

Too often we overlook the small miracles that happen in our daily lives, while we're waiting for that big thing to happen; the miracle of waking each morning, taking that first breath of the day; the miracle of your baby's smile as she looks up at you with complete trust, or the touch of your spouse each night. Never overlook what God is doing in the little moments of your life. His love is all around you waiting for you to notice it. The women I described, and women like them all around the world are the "Quiet hero's" that our world needs more of. They are the hero's who are grateful for the little moments, thankful for God's presence in their life everyday. They recognize the miracles disguised as ordinary moments, and share who they are, and what they have with the world.

Do you see yourself in the outstanding women I've described so far? I hope so, because every woman has the potential to be outstanding, every woman has the ability to lead an amazing life. Every woman is special to God, and has access to him at all times. All the women I've described so far are very much like the women the author of Proverbs 31 spoke of in the Bible. I say women, and not woman because I believe that Proverbs 31 describes the best qualities in all women. The author highlights our potential for greatness in everyday life. It is believed that Solomon wrote proverbs, if that's the case he was surrounded by many women. He had the opportunity to witness first hand on a daily basis who women are in secret, who we are in public, and how we express love, and faith. Solomon had a wondrous gift of being able to see past the superficial, and observe the heart. Proverbs 31 is an observation of the amazing heart of a woman.

-Proverbs 31-

" A good woman is hard to find, and worth far more than diamonds. Her husband trusts her without reserve, and never has reason to regret it...She's up before dawn, preparing breakfast for her family And organizing her day...She senses the worth of her work, is in no hurry to call it quits for the day. She's quick to assist anyone in need, reaches out to help the poor...When she speaks she always has something worthwhile to say And always says it kindly... Charm can mislead and beauty soon fades. The woman to be admired and Praised is the woman who lives in the Fear-of-God. Give her everything she deserves! Festoon her life with praise!"

"AN OUTSTANDING WOMAN" Poem by Tori Vigil

An Outstanding Woman is of timeless grace

> *A woman of virtue*

> *A woman who prays*

An Outstanding Woman is one who believes

> *She's not afraid to claim Christ as her king*

> *She lives to bring honor to His holy name*

> *She's virtuous, humble, grateful and brave*

An Outstanding Woman is a beacon of light

> *Her beauty shines from deep within*

> *She's eager to give of her time & talents*

> *She's willing to share her knowledge and faith*

An Outstanding woman is a woman of vision

> *She lives for today*

> *She prepares for tomorrow*

> *And she's learned to let go of yesterday*

She's a leader; A wife & a Mother

> *A Friend & a Daughter*

> *And with Gods help she paves the way for the future!*

By Tori Vigil

I chose to write about the outstanding women in this book not necessarily for what they've done, but because of what God has done for them. They first and foremost love and serve Christ, making God the first priority in their lives, and family the second most important. When God is at the center of your life all the other things just fall into their rightful place. Perhaps some of you reading this book right now do not feel that way. It is not easy to believe in a God you cannot see, love a God you may not feel, or trust a God you may not know. However, the women in this book will tell you that they would not have made it through the struggles of their past without faith in the Creator of the Universe. Their faith in a God that loved them the way they were, provided for them even when they thought they didn't deserve it, and blessed them beyond their imagination. That is why they are where they are today. I believe that we are all created equal, all created in God's image, and all filled with God's grace. When we find our purpose in this life all things we need to fulfill that purpose will also fall into place. A life lived with purpose is a life well lived, regardless of where you live, what you get paid, what your title is, or if you're well known.

Purpose (a sense of meaning and significance) is the driving force for all human beings. If you ask someone what they want out of life no matter what answer they give you, or how differently they word it, the underlying reason will be that they want to know they have a purpose. They want a reason for being here, and for their life to have significance. That purpose, that divine reason for being is what I hope to inspire you to find and develop for yourself, it's my reason for writing this book.

When I came to that moment in my own life when I finally knew why God created me, what my purpose was, and that it could help others; I felt complete, whole, and happy in a way that's hard to explain. I found my true self. I defined my own womanhood based on how God saw me, and I embraced the destiny he had for me. In embracing your God given destiny you are on the path of purpose and God is walking with you every step of the way. Everyone comes to a point in their life at sometime when they ask: who am I? Why am I here? What is my purpose? When you find the answer to these universal questions, your life will change forever. When you know who you are, then no obstacles that come up in your life can deter you from who you really are, and who God created you to be.

Patanjali once said that "when you are inspired by some great purpose, some extraordinary project, all your thoughts break their bonds; your mind transcends limitations, your consciousness expands in every direction, and you find yourself in a new, great and wonderful world. Dormant forces, faculties, and talents become alive and you discover yourself to be a greater person by far than you ever dreamed yourself to be."

Most of us today let others define who we are, and what we should be. The problem with that is very often others define us based on their values, beliefs, and past experiences. Since all of those factors are vastly different from one person to another, everyone will have a different definition of who they think you should be. You can not please everyone, so why try, simply please yourself and God. God already laid out a blue print of success in the Bible. Despite what you may have learned as a child God doesn't want to control your life, rather than defining you he wants to guide you to discover your unlimited potential. He wants to be a partner with you in this life, so that working together you can fulfill your purpose and make a difference. Don't live your entire life without knowing who you are, or why you are here.

Wayne Dyer, one of my favorite speakers said that your life purpose is a great gift. It is like a piece of music within you waiting to be shared with the world, so don't die with your music still in you. Rick Warren, one of my favorite authors, said that "without a purpose life is motion without meaning, activity without direction, and events without a reason. The greatest tragedy is not death, but life without a purpose."

Most human beings usually take the criticisms, opinions, and suggestions of others, and filter them through their our own past experiences. That often leads to offense, hurt feelings, re-gret, or it can fuel your determination to succeed. But why try to filter life based on the past. The past does not exist anymore except in your memories. If you've learned something from your past then it helped you grow, and therefore it was a good past, see it that way no matter what happened.

Now, in this moment, simply be yourself; define your own life based on your current values, beliefs, and your future expecta-tions of how you want your life to be, and what God is bringing into your life. When you view all of life's experiences in this way, then every action you take, every decision you make will take you closer to the life you desire, and the success that will ultimately come when you are functioning in your God given destiny. If you don't like your current values, and beliefs then hopefully the information in this book can help you change them to be more positive, and in line with Gods good plan for your life.

The power behind an outstanding life

You may be surprised to learn that God doesn't require that we be perfect. Proverbs 31 and other scriptures that portray women as these wonderful creatures simply capture our wonderful moments. I've seen some women get upset with this scripture, believing that it says men should expect perfection from us. I've never seen this scripture in this way. We all have moments of great success, and moments of great weakness. I believe this scripture is trying to get all people to focus on the great moments of success, to remember the times in our lives when we do good things. So that way when the weak moments come, we can get through them, not dwell on them, or get stuck in them.

In those weak moments we often feel foolish. It's in those weak moments when we as women often experience strong emotions, and deep seated thoughts; like we don't feel good enough, smart enough, talented enough, or beautiful enough. Yet God loves us through those moments; and when those moments are over, we come to our senses about how blessed we really are, and God is glorified. We are only human, and as humans we will make mistakes, we will make bad choices, and we will experience anger. So knowing that those moments will come to all humans, when they do come, remember that it is how you respond to those moments that make you who you are. Remember also, that even the greatest spiritual beings from the past, and present have gone through moments like that.

1 Corinthians 1:27 (KJV)

For God has chosen the foolish things of the world to confound the wise, and God has chosen the weak things of the world to confound the mighty.

1Corinthians 1:27 (The Message)

Take a good look, friends at who you were. I don't see the brightest and the best among you, not many influential, not many from high-society families. Isn't it obvious that God deliberately chose these people (women) that the culture overlooks and exploits and abuses, chose these "nobodies" to expose the hollow pretensions of the "somebodies"? ...Everything we have – right thinking, and right living, a clean slate and a fresh start – comes from God by way of Jesus Christ.

Look back at the most outstanding women you can think of, lets say Mother Teresa for example. She was a very small woman in stature. Just by looking at her you might assume she was very fragile, but she became a very influential person. She changed the lives of many people simply by caring for one person at a time. What I love most about Mother Teresa, is that she wasn't afraid to admit her mistakes, and change course. Then there was Ann Frank, Harriet Tubman, Helen Keller, and most recently Hillary Clinton, along with many others.

These women became a big part of history because their strength came from within, from a faith in a God they knew would never abandon them no matter what. They took something they liked to do, something they believed in, and let it become their passion. They expressed that passion one moment at a time, to one person at a time. Though none of these women were perfect (who could ever be) each woman put a crack in the glass ceiling of what the world thought women could accomplish, and they made the way easier for the rest of us.

Mother Teresa had a passion for helping others and showing them God's love; Ann Frank had a passion for life, and she wrote about it even though she thought no one would be interested in reading it later on; Harriet Tubman had a passion for freedom; Helen Keller had a passion for words, Hillary Clinton and had a passion for America. As children and even as they got older, all of these women may have easily been overlooked by their culture, and been seen as nobodies; and what of the most blessed woman in history, Mary – Mother of Jesus. She was a very young girl just like any other girl in the town where she lived. Not even she herself understood why God had chosen her to give birth to His son. Hillary Clinton's mother was born in a time when women couldn't even vote, yet Hillary's daughter voted for her mother to be President. How amazing that God has brought women up to a place of such high esteem. God saw greatness in these women, and he see's it in you too. Many people over the years have asked what these women must have felt at their moments of opportunity. How did Harriet Tubman feel while helping other slaves escape to freedom; how did Mary the mother of Jesus feel when she accepted the angel's words that she would give birth to the Son-of-God? One might think they felt honored to be able to take part in such great service, but I think they must have felt great fear. Both Harriet and Mary could have been killed for their decisions.

"Courage is not the absence of fear, but rather the judgment that something else is more important than fear"

-Ambrose Redmoon-

It was only by Gods grace these women were able to accomplish the things they did. Have you ever wondered what Grace really is? I've come to know grace as the kindness, and forgiveness of God that shows through in your life on a daily basis. Grace in the simple things that only you would notice. Grace is the God given strength to say no to sin, and yes to destiny; the strength to accomplish your purpose on this earth in the face of great adversity. Grace gets you through your valleys, and over the mountain tops.

God truly has a special place in his heart for women. God spoke first to Mary before he spoke to Joseph, and Jesus proved it countless times as well, when he defended Mary Magdalene for pouring perfume on his feet; when he took so much time out of his day, and spoke to the woman at the well. By involving women in his ministry; when he appeared first to the women at his tomb after the resurrection. The greatness God saw in these women, he also sees in you. You have the ability to love unconditionally, to feel things profoundly, and to express yourself in genuine and powerful ways that can be felt by others. It was no accident either, God made you this way. You are an expression of his character. What an honor to be able to say that you were made in the image of your God.

One of my favorite women to read about in the Bible is Deborah. We first meet Deborah in the Book of Judges in an account of a battle where she led the soldiers of Israel, this battle occurred around 1050 BC. She is a true heroine in the Lord, and a wonderful example of just how we can answer the Lord's call on our lives. Her calling was not a typical one; she was a woman in leadership in the time of a male dominated world. Perhaps many women today can relate to her. Careful study of her story might just challenge the typical human assumptions about what, and who we can be as women, and as human beings. It is my hope that her story will also inspire all women to look to what God has gifted us to do, and be.

Judges 4:1-4 The Israelites again did what was evil in the sight of the Lord, after Ehud died. So the Lord sold them into the hand of King Jabin of Canaan, who reigned in Hazor; the commander of his army was Sisera, who lived in Harosheth-hagoiim. Then the Israelites cried out to the Lord for help; for he had nine hundred chariots of iron, and had oppressed the Israelites cruelly twenty years.

"At that time Deborah, a prophetess, wife of Lappidoth, was judging Israel."

Deborah was not only a gifted prophetess, but also a judge; two very prominent positions for a woman to hold in Israel at that time. As you read on the story says that through Deborah God gave victory to the army of Israel. Imagine being a woman in those times, and having to lead an entire army of men into battle against odds that looked like sure death. Today we may not face an army, but each of us face some storm, some hardship. Deborah had to be brave, she had to be confident as she stood before an army of men probably twice the size of her army, and she had to have faith that God would fulfill his promises. Do you know what promises God has made to you? Do you have faith to believe God is faithful to fulfill those promises in your life? Deborah's kind of faith, and positive thinking is what I hope you will find for yourself. I also hope you learn much more in reading about the successes, struggles, and miracles that have happened in these women's lives.

Personal Notes

Chapter Two

Tori Vigil

In the image of a creative God

Galatians 6:1,4-5 (the Message bible)

Live creatively friends...Make a careful exploration of which you

are, and the work you have been given, and then sink yourself into

that... Each of you must take responsibility for doing the creative

best you can with your own life.

Photo courtesy of Tori Vigil

"We are all creative beings,

The key is to connect with the source of creativity,

The creator of the universe"

-Tori Vigil-

Have you ever thought that some people were just born crea-tive, and others were not? What if you were in a group setting, and you were asked to talk about the ways you are creative; would you have a lot to say, or would you struggle to think of something? I admire creative women: women who are photog-raphers, painters, writers, singers, designers, women who knit or sow, or are good at crafts.

Yet many women sometimes claim that they just aren't creative at all.

A friend of mine once said she must have been absent the day God handed out creativity. That couldn't be farther from the truth. We are all created in God's image, and God is a creative being. It's just a matter of tapping into that creative energy within, and all around you. Unlocking your creativity will open your world to many new things. It is freeing, and stress reduc-ing simply being creative, whether at work, at play, or in minis-try. There are many ways to show the creativity of our Heavenly Father. Creativity goes beyond the well known artistic styles that people normally consider as creative.

Creativity is: keeping a budget, meeting people's needs, juggling relationships, showing kindness, running a ministry or a business, or raising children. All of this takes creative energy to accomplish, and be successful at it. Mother Teresa once said "we are all pencils in the hand of God". Well if God is writing a song or drawing a picture then we are the tools he's chosen to use. You let creativity shine when you step out of the box, break out of the mold, and choose to stand out from society at large. You let creativity shine when you choose to let your actions and your life reflect Jesus Christ.

It was not so long ago when I lived a life of chaos and uncertainty, but my life has changed for the better. I am a positive person, living a creative life, and my dreams are coming true every day. I'd like to share with you the secret that lead me on the path of my purpose.

-DEEPAK CHOPRA-

"Beneath the layers of chaos, and uncertainty
something creative is always happening."

Choose to live creatively everyday! By that I mean choose to think creatively, feel creative, and take creative actions every day. Practice creativity any chance you get. Be creative at work, at home, and in the little things. I know it is not always an easy thing to remain in a passionate, creative vibration. Distractions come, life happens, and you have bad days. We are after all only human, and life has a way of being a roller coaster ride.

The key to living a creative life is to realize that all life is constantly in motion, therefore it's constantly changing. Nothing can exist on our planet if it is not changing. You can choose to not let bad days, distractions, or unexpected circumstances put you on a path to negativity, but rather learn from them. See each trial, problem, and circumstance as an opportunity for change, and make that change a positive and affirming one.

-DWIGHT EISENHOWER-

"No one can defeat us unless we first defeat ourselves"

I've come to learn that sometimes we are our own worst critics, our own worst enemy. Often times we defeat ourselves by our own thinking. If you look back at your past at your most successful moments, why were they a success? In my own life I know I would initially say those moments were a success due to determination, and hard work; but looking deeper they were successful because I believed they would be successful. Looking back at the moments that were not what I wanted them to be, why were they not a success? Initially you want to blame; it was my bosses fault, I just had a bad day, I was off my game, or it was because that person just didn't like me. But looking deeper than that, past the superficial reasons/excuses, it was because I had doubt in those moments. I didn't have confidence in myself, in who God created, so it was my own thinking that defeated me.

Thoughts are powerful things indeed, and when our thoughts are combined with our emotions they become even more powerful, then when we speak them out loud our thoughts create things. I believe that we are all created in the image of a creative God, and therefore the power of creativity already resides in each of us. God spoke the world into existence; his words have power, and so do ours. I actually spoke about this topic on an episode of my radio show. I know that not everyone will share my beliefs in a creative God, but I hope that you can still take away the main point of this message, which is that you are a creative being, whose thoughts and words have creative power!

-*WINSTON CHURCHILL*-

"You create your own universe as you go along."

What I've learned to do over the years is start each day being thankful for the many blessings God has given me. Thankfulness and gratitude start the path of my day on a positive note, I then pray. I grew up watching my grandmother pray every night before she went to bed. I used to love spending the weekends at her house. I'd put on her oversize pajamas that practically swallowed me, then we'd kneel beside her bed, she'd hold her rosary, and we'd pray. She would pray for every member of our family (which usually took hours because we have a very large family). It amazed me that she was so dedicated to all of us; that she thought of all of us every night. It was she that taught me the power, and importance of being a praying woman.

In addition to prayer, I also have a vision journal. Many people use vision boards, but I found that didn't work well for me. I always have my journal around, and use it all day long everyday, so a journal rather than something hanging on the wall works well for me. I've always been a very visual person, and seeing things in my journal helps me to remember, and focus; so I look at the images, and words I have on my vision journal every day. I speak the words out load as I pray daily, and I am grateful for each item I've listed in my vision journal. As I pray, focus, and show gratitude for the things I've listed, I am also fully expecting those things to come into my life. I am not afraid to ask for what I want, and what I need. But I have to say that it's a little more than just asking God to bless me, it's a knowing that what I want also wants me. God wants to bless me, because he wants me to be a blessing. This kind of knowing produces a faith without doubts. I've already seen many of my requests answered. Below I've listed some of the things that have been a part of my vision journals.

-John 16:24-

"Until now you have not asked for anything in my name. Ask and you will receive, and your joy will be complete"

Prayerful Affirmations – (Think and say these things)

I agree with God's word which says I am victorious in all things, and that I am more than a conqueror, through Jesus!

Wealth and prosperity are coming my way; so as to establish Gods covenant on this earth, and for the benefit of everyone involved.

I can be certain in uncertain times because I am not connected to the economy of this world—or the rules of their house. I am connected to God's economy—the rules of His house. I live by the system of sowing and reaping.

Something good is going to happen for me, to me, or through me today. Things are going to work out. God has a good plan for my life today. He is certain that it is good;

therefore I'm certain as well.

I expect divine favor in my life today. Just as with David, God's favor surrounds me like a shield. God is opening doors for me that no one can close.

God is going to right every wrong from my past, and show the same help to me as He did for Moses, Abraham, Isaac and Jacob. He gives me wisdom and holds nothing back. I'm in the front of the line.

I know that faith works, I also know that my faith works by refusing to hold anything against anyone (we reap what we sow). When praying I choose to forgive because forgiveness is the gateway to answered prayer.

I remember the many good things that God has already done throughout history, and therefore I know he will do good again, in fact I expect Him to do it again. Good and right things are going to happen in my life today!

I will focus on what's happening in me rather than to me.

All is well and I can feel a deep calm within me,

And even under that, a joy, a deep joy,

In being who I am and in living this life, just as it is.

Just as I am, here and now, I am exactly right.

This is how it is meant to be right now,

And the action that I take in this moment,

From this place of peace and joy deeply centered within,

Will always be the best possible action,

For myself and for the unfolding of purpose,

For me and the others involved in my life,

And even those I may never meet.

Being positive, affirming, asking for things, and believing I'll get them has not always been easy for me. I know that I am not the only woman on the planet who had a hard time asking for things. Part of our fear of asking for things comes from lack of confidence, fear of rejection, and that we don't want to be perceived as needy or greedy. If you truly need or want what you are asking for, then you must ask as if you believe you will get it because you deserve it. People don't like to give to someone who either won't appreciate what they give, or will waste what they give you. However, people love to give to those who are appreciative, and use what they give for a purpose. People like to be a part of something positive and affirming.

Tori's Story

I've always considered myself to be creative. My father was a painter, and a musician, and inspired me to be creative since I was young. But my real creativity started when I got older, when Jesus came into my life. I stood there in this new church, listening to the music with such amazement when suddenly I felt the baby in my womb kick for the first time. Looking down at my belly I put my hand on the spot where I felt the movement, and the baby kicked again. I looked into the eyes of my husband, grabbed his hand and put it on my belly. The look on his face said he felt it too, and we both new the baby was feeling the same thing we were feeling. God was in this place.

That was my first experience going to a non-catholic church. I had never seen a service like that, never heard a preacher like that, and I never imagined that people actually danced in church. But I knew what I felt, and it was at that moment I decided that I wanted this God to be a part of my life forever. In that moment, I asked Jesus to be my Lord, and Savior.

Since that day I've had many moments of inspiration which have motivated me to write, sing, speak, paint, and capture God's creativity through photography. Having three daughters also presented me with many opportunities to be creative. Though sometimes it took a little effort and research, as well as time to learn new things.

Creativity in all its forms has many purposes, but when it's used in a way to communicate with God, or allow God to communicate to the world through us it can be a powerful tool. Creativity in all its forms can express: faith, hope, love, passion, pain, forgiveness, healing, and the list could go on. What I would like to share with you is how God can use creativity to heal us. Very often we need to allow healing to take place in different areas of our lives be it our emotions, our thoughts, or our physical bodies. Trauma survivors often find it hard to talk about their traumatic experience; however survivors all over the world are using creativity to find healing from a painful past. Whether it is healing from physical or psychological traumas, survivors are making their way through the various stages of recovery using some form of creativity.

Taking the path of healing through creativity helps to stop the feelings of abandonment, undeserved guilt, and the fear that causes a person to remain silent, often felt by survivors. By expressing their internal pain through a positive focused activity they release part of that pain which then opens their hearts again to allow healing to take place. Over the years I've developed a simple 8 step program to help people heal through creativity. It's so exciting to see God at work in peoples lives.

Ever find it hard to express your emotions? As a child that was the hardest thing for me to do. Though my emotions often overwhelmed me, I feared letting them show. You see even though I grew up in a creative atmosphere it was also a dysfunctional one. I was hit, molested by extended family members, ridiculed by people at school, and put in many harmful situations. The hardest part of all this was that it was people I trusted, who should have been caring for me that ended up hurting me the most. I carried bitterness; anger, hate, and regret in my heart for a long time, and it ate away at me as if it were a disease. It was a great load for such a young woman to carry; such disturbing memories for anyone to have to bear.

One specific memory is when I was a child. The smell of smoke hung thick in the air and even though I was in my room with the door shut I could still smell it, even taste it. It was that familiar scent of Marijuana mixed with tobacco. This scene was almost a nightly occurrence at my home during my father's drunken parties with his friends. These memories go back as far as I can remember. I'd lie in bed quietly listening to what was being said, the curse words being used to tell ridiculous stories of bar fights, and drunken car crashes. I'd lie in bed waiting for someone to walk down the hallway mistaking my bedroom door for the bathroom, and barging in on my sisters sleeping. It always happened, so I always waited for it.

Our door didn't have a lock, and my father refused to put one on the door, so when I heard someone clumsily tripping his way to the restroom I'd grab the door handle holding it shut as tight as I could. They would struggle with it a moment then move onto the next door, and for the moment I'd be relieved. They would all eventually leave trying to make their way to their own houses, or they'd fall asleep on the sofa, or the floor, when I was sure it was safe I'd let myself drift off to sleep. Usually two to four hours later I'd be awakened by my mother to get ready for school. Needless to say sleep deprivation was a normal part of my life.

My dad wasn't always the mean tyrant I feared, there were times when he was sober, and like many other normal dads he would sing us to sleep, and teach us to fish, hunt, and work the farm. But for me those times were few and far between, when they came I cherished them, they were a ray of sunshine that held me over during the storms. But nothing could comfort me when another family member turned his unwanted affections toward me. I was scared, alone, and no longer myself at those times. I felt so ashamed, embarrassed, helpless, and every time it happened I felt less and less like a person. The abuse went on for years. I had been robbed of innocence, trust in mankind, and hope. When my father eventually found out he didn't believe me, he took that person's side and I was shunned by my entire family.

When I found a friend in the only person of the opposite sex that I felt I could trust, I gave everything I had to him. I found comfort in his voice, and safety in his arms. He wasn't like the other men in my life, the men I had grown up around. He wasn't like the drunkards who grabbed at me under the table, or as they walked by me. He was sweet and there was a peace, and calmness about him, I clung to him as if he was my only way of escape.

The crazy thing about abuse is

That it leaves you so confused about yourself afterward.

You make choices that another person,

Who has never been abused, just can't understand.

You loose the trust in your own choices and detach yourself

emotionally

So you don't have to feel the hurt;

It becomes a habit that stays with you for a long time.

It affects all other relationships in your life.

I told him my secrets, shared with him my hidden shame, and he took me away from this life of fear. He was the first man I ever trusted. I was very young when I got pregnant, then we moved out on our own, and eventually we got married. We lived with my mother-in-law for awhile, then roomed with my brother-in-law, and eventually were able to get our own place.

Life really can be difficult on its own when you're an adult, but it's even more so when you're trying to live a normal adult life as a teenager. I know we wouldn't have survived in our marriage had it not been for the help, and support of a wonderful couple in a great church that took us under their wing. They taught us to communicate with each other, to make compromises, to make our choices based on God's word and our love for each other. They told us the most important factor to keeping a marriage alive is to have fun. In the church, and in God I found a place of peace, hope, faith, and forgiveness. I found it in my heart to forgive, and to mend the relationship with my parents. I can now say both I and my parents are grateful for the connection we now share.

I read a quote once that has stuck with me
"Forgive every body everything Accept the past as past
Without denying it or discarding it.
Reminisce about it, but don't live in it,

Learn from it, but don't punish yourself about it

or continually regret it. And don't get stuck in it."

Forgiveness can be a very hard thing to give, and sometimes a very hard thing to receive as well. It was hard to say that I forgive my abuser for what he did to me, that I forgive myself for not telling someone about what was going on. That I forgive my parents for failing me, and that I forgive my father for the life he exposed me to. But forgiveness was the next and very important step I needed to take in my healing process. For so long all the bitterness, anger, and resentment had sat in me like a virus; it had been growing in strength, eating away at my spirit. I needed to heal from that and forgiveness was the only way to recovery.

Psalm 25:11

"For the sake of your name, O Lord,

forgive my iniquity, though it is great."

As anger grows, it makes you feel as if the person you are angry with owes you something; guilt makes you feel as if you owe someone else something; and regret makes you feel as if you owe yourself something. When a debt is owed there are only two ways to get rid of it, pay it off or forgive it. Forgiveness does not erase what they did; it simply releases everyone from having to pay it back. If I had continued to hold onto those debts, I would have been waiting for the rest of my life to be paid, and of course that wasn't going to happen. When you really think about it you have to put a value on what is owed to you, and what could my abuser do to pay me for the loss of confidence, the loss of trust in myself and others? A debt like that can never be paid. The Lord did not want me to wait around to be paid, he wanted me to forgive and leave vengeance to the Him. God says it belongs to him anyway.

Forgiveness was my path to healing,

And after I forgave, I felt complete for the first time in my life.

Through Christ's love I am now a whole person,

By Tori Vigil

Redeemed and able to help others.

The Lord will always take what the enemy meant for evil

And use it for our good.

For others I've met healing came a different way; through poetry, drawing, music, pottery, and other creative works. For me forgiveness came through the act of creative writing. The Lord laid it upon my heart to write my life story in book form. For five years I argued with God. Giving Him every excuse I could think of as to why I shouldn't have to write a book, why I didn't want anyone knowing about my past especially my daughters. After five years of debating with God, I realized God wasn't changing His mind, so I finally decided to be obedient. It was a hard process, but just getting all my emotions out, and having to express them in words I knew others would read was very healing. I had to identify what the emotion was, and what caused it. In the end I had a marvelous book, and healing from my past. I created photographs and paintings to express my emotions, and one of them became the cover to my book "Surviving the Teenage Journey". God brought a wonderful woman into my life who was also a publisher. I submitted the book proposal to her, and her daughter found the proposal on her desk. Based on the reaction of her daughter, the publisher decided to go ahead and publish the book, and a friendship was formed. It is amazing how God works everything together for our good.

Romans 8:28

"And we know that all things work together for good
to those who love God, to those who are the called according
to His purpose."

The results from your creative work may just take you completely by surprise. I know it did me. I've read letters, and had conversations with many women young and old alike who say they've been touched by what I wrote in my book. That by far is the greatest reward of all. We may not be able to change the world, but we can make a difference by touching the life of one person at a time. When I was younger I never thought I'd be a writer, a speaker, an author, a photographer, or a radio talk show host, but God has greatly blessed me indeed.

I've attended many Take Back the Night rallies, and other events like it where I have heard many women tell their stories of how they've overcome their pain. Creativity, by far has been the best healing process. By taking a simple step to use some-thing creative that they enjoyed doing, and letting it become their passion some women have done extraordinary things. Some have written wonderful poems, or created amazing paint-ings. Some women have written books like I did, and others have started some extraordinary ministries that reach out to other women. One such woman comes to mind her name is Victoria Kelly, and she is the founder of A.H.H.H.S. (A Helping Hand for Healing Souls); or another friend of mine Loretta (Medicine Sky Woman) who is the founder of T.A.T.A.N. (The Angel to Angel Network). Yet other women have used their creativity to volunteer for existing organizations in many areas of need. Whatever your creative force may be don't be afraid to use it for the Glory of God our Father; after all, you are made in the image of a Creative God.

Personal Notes

_____

_____

_____

_____

_____

_____

_____

_____

_____

_____

_____

_____

Chapter Three
J'Lynn Howle

Today's Woman Leader

Mark 10:43

"Whoever wants to be a leader among you

must be your servant"

By Tori Vigil

Photo courtesy of J'Lynn Howle

"My Boss is a Jewish Carpenter"

Colossians 3:23

"Whatever you do, work at it with all your heart

as working for the Lord, not for men"

Today's Women Leaders

As I started to write this chapter, I began to analyze how I felt about, and what I thought about the leadership roles of women today, and in the future. I thought about leadership roles women have in government, family, business, and spirituality. I immediately assumed that in a work, and ministry environment there is still that glass ceiling, and not very many women in leadership roles today (at least not as many as I'd like to see). So I tested that assumption, and started doing some research. Did you know that in 1991 the government decided to do some research of their own? They started keeping track of *The Glass Ceiling.* That is to say that they wanted to know how many women were in leadership positions in America. According to Mary O'Sullivan Deputy Director of the CIA's office of policy support; Since 1991 women in executive leadership roles has doubled; women in top civil service leadership roles has more than doubled, and women in senior executive and civil service leadership roles has more than tripled.

Definitely some good news for women, but we still have a long way to go. In 1987 Wilma Mankiller was the first woman to become a chief in the Cherokee Nation; and according to the US Federal Labor Statistics from 2006 only 1 in every eight clergy members are women. I know that women are called of God to do his work, yet most of them are not being ordained, or standing behind the pulpit. There is still a great controversy about whether women are meant to be behind the pulpit, and in other leadership positions in the church. I happen to think that scripture answered that question a long time ago. Look at Esther (the queen of Persia), Deborah (a Judge over Israel), Lydia (one of the first females to share the gospel of Jesus), Mary (mother of Jesus, the first to see the angel). As I said in the introduction of this book Jesus raised women to higher levels of dignity and respect.

After listening to others, talking with others, and doing some research about what God says about women; I have found a list of the top 5 qualities of great women leaders. The top one is being a good listener. No matter what leadership role a woman may have, it will be hard to do great if you can't listen to those around you, and listen to what God is saying to you everyday. Listening is more than just hearing what is being said, but being aware of how others words affect you. Being compassionate to the validity of others feelings, wants, dreams, visions, and desires; being a good observer of people's body language.

The second is to be a good communicator. It can take time to learn how to communicate effectively with God, and with other people. I've always been good at communicating with the written word, but not so good at communicating with the spoken word; that took time for me to learn. It was not easy in the beginning to get up in front of an audience. I'd feel my knees shake, my stomach would ache, I'd get nauseous, and my palms get clammy. It was not easy when God told me to be a radio talk show host (believe me I debated with Him on that one too).

I'll share a little story with you. In high school I was a fairly good student, and was proud of that fact; but one year in social studies, I took my first "F" because part of our major grade involved getting up in front of the class to deliver a report we had written. I couldn't do it, I refused to do it, and I accepted my first "F". I will never forget how that experience made me feel. I vowed to never let fear get the better of me like that again. Sometimes in order to grow spiritually, and as a person you just have to face your fears.

Thirdly a great woman leader is an eternal student. A person should never stop learning, growing, being open to testing out new ideas, being mentally agile, or being adaptable to change. Being a student is being someone who reads, examines things, is curious, and seeks out answers. Jesus' disciples are the perfect example of great students. They were so eager to just sit at his feet; and soak up his knowledge, ask him questions, try out new ways of doing things, and new ways of thinking.

Fourthly a great woman leader has a great moral compass. She is honest and fair; knows her values, morals, and belief system. You've probably heard the old saying, "if you don't believe in something then you'll fall for anything". You have to start with a good foundation. For Christian women that foundation is Gods word, and his truth. A great woman leader makes her decisions in all areas of life based on her core values.

The fifth quality of a great woman leader is someone who knows who they are. Get to know who God says you are. Get to know what your gifts, talents, abilities, strengths, weaknesses, passions, and unique qualities are. God made you the way you are for a reason. Everything about you is a gift, be thankful for those gifts, and be willing to share them with the world, and with your family. Knowing who you are involves being able to balance, and integrate all areas of your life; work, family, health, and spirituality. By integrate I mean allowing all areas in your life to mesh together in perfect harmony; so that you can get things done, but do it with love, joy, and at the right time.

The young ladies in the past really didn't have many women in leadership roles they could look to as role models. Well thank God that has changed. We have more of those female role models today. Women in leadership roles from the past, and women in the present, like J'Lynn Howle.

A Crown of Opportunity

What little girl hasn't sat in front of the TV watching the Miss America pageant, and dream of wearing that crown? Some little girls grow up to become amazing women who pursued that childhood dream of wearing a crown. J'Lynn was one of those women who found the opportunity to make it happen.

When I tried to imagine the lifestyle of Miss America, or any pageant queen, I had a certain perception, perhaps like you. I pictured fun, celebrities, and good times. I pictured women falling over each other to win, but the more I spoke with J'Lynn, the more I came to see a different side of the crown that most of us don't think about. We don't often think about all the behind the scenes stuff that goes with this job, because that's what wearing a crown is, a Job!

"Opportunity is often missed because it is dressed in overalls and looks like work." –Thomas Edison-

Thomas Edison was right, how often do we wish for wealth, or fame, or even to do something worth while. Yet when the opportunity arises it looks like so much work, we let it pass by because we don't want to set aside that much time. We don't want to work that hard. We don't think there's anything in it for us. Sometimes we don't think we're capable of doing the job.

Eventually, after wearing several crowns of her own, J'Lynn was presented with the opportunity to start her own company "Virtue International Pageants." When this opportunity came about she could have just seen the overalls (the hard work), and even more than that she could have only seen her inner fears and insecurities. Her childhood experiences, and hardships could have begun to creep back into her mind; and she would have been filled with doubts. Was she pretty enough, was she skinny enough, could she be a good speaker. Would wearing a crown go to her head, and make her different somehow, was she really capable of being a leader? Have you ever asked yourself those type of questions, when faced with a big opportunity?

Isn't it amazing how much we let fear control our lives. Fear of many things, and everyone has a fear of something. But when we let that fear influence our daily decisions, we give up control to it. We loose out on so many great and wonderful things, because of this emotion, and thought process called fear.

"It is fear that keeps people small,

so run toward your fears and embrace them.

Because on the other side of your greatest fears

is your greatest life."

-Robin Sharma-

You may, or may not have heard of Esther before; if not I'd like you to meet another young woman who overcame great fear, in the Bible, we find her in the book of Esther. This is an amazing story of a young girl who comes from a humble family, and is chosen to be the queen of Persia. At the end of this action packed drama, she is used by God. Through her faith, and courage God saves the entire nation of Israel from death. In a time when women were looked upon as nothing more than possessions; she captured the heart of a king. Because of their love, she gained a place of honor in his eyes which made it possible for her to save her people. Never underestimate the power of pure, unconditional love. Love can overcome fear, and bring hope of a bright future.

When we are able to overcome fear, and take back control of our destiny we can see what we've been missing out on. J'Lynn was really being presented with the opportunity to let her voice be heard; to let her beliefs, and convictions be made known in a much louder way than they could have been expressed before. She chose to take the opportunity that the universe gave to her, and is now a role model for women of all ages. What a great honor, and an awesome responsibility.

J'Lynn is a Mother of three wonderful children, William, Candi, and Dallas; she is the Wife to her high school sweetheart of over 28 years, and is the founder & CEO of "Virtue International Pageants". She is affectionately known as the founder of Christian pageantry. Gradually J'Lynn felt her calling begin to change, and after being in pageantry for over 20 years; as a competitor, judge, and director of "Virtue International Pageants" which has had great success having produced several exiting pageants each year; In 1992 J'Lynn became an ordained minister and currently travels all over the country sharing her story with women; and she is soon to publish a memoir of her life.

J'Lynn's passion for Christian women is to give them well deserved honor, and recognition for their commitments to marriage, family, moral character, and personal achievements. According to Proverbs 31:31 "give her the recognition she deserves, and let her works Bring her praise". That was a tough concept for me to wrap my head around. I was always taught that women should be modest, stay out of the spotlight, not be haughty, not be proud. But I learned that it does not glorify God to stay in the shadows; to down play your talents, to refuse to live up to the potential He has placed within you. Sometimes God wants us to strut our stuff, not in a haughty way, but to say look what God did for me, because he wants to do it for you too. J'Lynn shared with me that when the crown comes off; she, and other pageant queens are women like you and me. They are not just about beauty; they have substance, values, convictions, beliefs, goals, and visions for a brighter tomorrow. They are well educated, serve in the community, strongly believe in their platforms, and are multi-talented. Many of the young pageant queens I had the opportunity to meet are simply amazing; I found them to be hard workers who even at their young age, knew what they wanted out of life, and were striving to reach their goals. So here's a big applaud to all the reigning queens, queens-to-be, and the queens of every father's heart, you are outstanding. Believe in yourself and don't let the fear of loosing keep you from going for what you want, or dream; it's not about winning it's about getting to know yourself better, growing, and becoming better than you were yesterday. It's about sharing your story with others, being a source of encouragement, and a source of hope to others.

The Crowns of Heaven

As a Christian woman, J'Lynn believes that you can be a virtuous Christian woman in pageantry, at your job, with your family, and in every part of your life. Although she's given many crowns to various women over the years, she says it is the crowns of heaven we should be valuing most of all and those crowns are available to every Christian. That started me wondering, what are the crowns of heaven?

"Everyone who competes for the prize is temperate (self controlled) in all things. Now they do it to obtain a perishable crown, but we do it for an imperishable crown."

- 1 Corinthians 9:25-

There are many ways to be awarded on this earth such as with beautiful crowns of gold, medals we can wear around our necks, or degrees we can hang on the wall; all of these things given to us for the many roles we women play. But all those things eventually fade away; gold looses its shimmer, medals are forgotten, degrees on the wall don't change who we really are. A Christian woman can look forward to the greater rewards that come from her heavenly father. Those rewards are eternal, and imperishable. So enjoy the awards given on earth but remember to look forward to the crowns that last. Scripture lists for us which crowns really matter and I'd like to share them with you now. It was Denzel Washington who once said that *"Man gives the award, God gives the reward."*

The Crown of Life

"Consider it pure joy, my brothers, whenever you face trials of many kinds, because you know that the testing of your faith develops perseverance. Blessed is the man who perseveres under trial, because when he has stood the test, he will receive the crown of life that God has promised to those who love him" (James 1:2-3, 12).

The crown of life is a promise of eternal life given to those that love, honor, and trust God while here on this earth. It is given to those who remain faithful through all of life's joys and sorrows. We have many chances during our journey through life to turn our back on God. At times turning our back on God seems like the easier thing to do, especially when life seems to have more heartache than we can bear, fear that overwhelms us, and great obstacles that we must over come. It is not always easy to follow a God you can not see, love a God you can not feel, and hope in a future you are unsure of; but for those who do follow and love and dare to hope, what a wondrous crown awaits them at the end of their journey, and what great joys they will find on the way.

"You can always tell how blessed you will be tomorrow based on how much struggle you are going through today."

—Bishop George Bloomer-

The Crown of Righteousness

"I have fought the good fight, I have finished the race, and I have kept the faith. Now there is in store for me the crown of righteousness, which the Lord, the righteous Judge, will award to me on that day — and not only to me, but also to all who have longed for his appearing" (2 Timothy 4:7-8).

Righteousness -Put simply it is the rightness of God. It is relationship with God and with God's people (because God is in his people); it is also the process of becoming like Christ.

The crown of righteousness is given to those that stay focused on the big picture, sharing Gods love with the world. It is a crown for those who fight the good fight, by remaining faithful, boldly sharing Christ's story with others. This is not always an easy thing to do. It takes boldness to share your faith and be-liefs with today's self sufficient society who don't think they need a God. Yet if you share Christ with one person at a time, through one relationship at a time then you help them realize that they are all searching for something.

That something is a relationship with a real and relevant God, our heavenly father. We all need to be connected to the source of life. Some people spend a lifetime searching for what they think will make them happy; complete; give their life purpose, and meaning. Those who have found true happiness will tell you it can not be found, if you focus on yourself. Happiness comes when you live your life in service to others. To see joy on another person's face because you took the time to care; to know peace, and contentment because you gave someone else's life meaning; to feel the deep embrace of a child as they thank you for feeding them; those are life's greatest rewards.

"No man is useless who lightens the burdens of another"

- Charles Dickens-

The Crown of Glory

"Shepherd the flock of God which is among you, serving as overseers, not by compulsion but willingly, not for dishonest gain but eagerly; nor as being lords over those entrusted to you, but being examples to the flock; and when the Chief Shepherd appears, you will receive the crown of glory that does not fade away" (1 Peter 5:2-4, NKJV).

The crown of Glory is given to those who lead, shepherd, teach, care for others, and help God's people through life's journey. It need not be in a huge way such as a pastor does; but it could be leading, and teaching your children; leading those who work for you, or caring for those who can not care for themselves. You can shepherd a flock if you're a leader in your job, and even if you're not in leadership you can still teach others through the way you live your life.

Ever wonder why God uses only some people to accomplish His will in big ways? We wonder things like this because we have been conditioned by society that only the big things matter. "The bigger the better", but if you read the bible from cover to cover, you'll see it's full of spectacular stories about how God works in people's lives. You'll see He works in the little things, the everyday things. God works in one person at a time through one act of obedience at a time. When people allow God's purposes to work through their lives in the little things, that's when the big things happen!

"Without a purpose, life is motion without meaning, activity without direction, and events without reason. The greatest tragedy is not death, but life without purpose" –Rick Warren-

The Crown of Rejoicing

"For what is our hope, or joy, or crown of rejoicing? Is it not even you in the presence of our Lord Jesus Christ at His coming? For you are our glory and joy (1 Thessalonians 2:19-20 NKJV)

"Happiness is when what you think, what you say and what you do, are all in harmony" –Gandhi said that. The crown of rejoicing is given to those that preach the gospel to the lost. Those who know that we can take nothing with us to heaven except other people. Did you know joy, happiness, and rejoicing are mentioned over 800 times in the bible? If God took the time to tell us over 800 times to be happy and rejoice than he must really mean it; it must be important to him. Contrary to what some people think Jesus was not always a very serious deity. He laughed with his disciples, he showed them love, and compassion; he rejoiced in the beautiful things life offers us.

"Success is the expansion of happiness" —Deepak Chopra-

J'Lynn's Story

Now that you know about J'Lynn's success in life; I'd like to share with you how she came about achieving that success. If you were to speak to J'Lynn in person, or even over the phone, you can hear the excitement in her voice as she paints for you a word picture of what her vision is for her company, and for her life. Excitement like that is very contagious, and it's easy to see why she is so successful. After looking over all that she has done, and accomplished throughout her life, you'd probably never imagine she would have had a horrible childhood. Often we only see the beautiful package of a successful life, never the obstacles people had to overcome to get there.

J'Lynn, and her younger siblings endured a very long childhood full of neglect, abandonment, perversion, and abuse. At one point their step father offered them up for sale to any one who would pay. J'Lynn's memories are filled with moments of great sorrow. The horrific memories started with the abuse of her younger siblings which quickly escalated to her own sexual abuse. Her step father pushed her into the world of human trafficking, and child pornography from the age of 12-17. A childhood such as this, so traumatic, would leave anyone with countless emotional, mental, and physical scars; scars that people carry with them for a lifetime. When I asked J'Lynn how it is that she overcome a childhood like that she said, "Only God has the power to heal your emotional problems, restore your life, and love you unconditionally."

J'Lynn took a great tragedy in her life, and made it a stepping stone. She took her pain, and made it her story; one that she tells others to help people overcome the same kind of past that she overcame. She allowed her wounds to give her wisdom.

When she looks at her scars, she sees how her life made a dramatic turn from going in the wrong direction to one of purpose. Often when you see someone who had a life like J'Lynn, one of two things happen, either they use the experience to build their purpose, or they let the experience eat away at them for the rest of their life. We sometimes carry the past with us, and it influences the way we see the world, our relationships, our self esteem, and our decisions.

I recently made a huge move with my family from Oregon to Colorado, and we towed a moving trailer behind our mini-van with our most precious possessions. The van barely crawled up the mountain passes at a snail speed of 20 miles per hour. Our little van worked so hard on that move. This is how life is for those who won't let go of the past. They tow their past with them wherever they go, and keep filling up that storage trailer as they go along until life in general just feels like an uphill struggle everyday. We only hold onto things that mean a lot to us, but those things may not necessarily be good for us. There comes a point when you want change. That change won't come unless you just get so tired of struggling that the need for change is stronger than the need to hold onto the past. When you get to that point, God make sure the universe provides the opportunity for change. Whether that change is good or bad will greatly depend on you, not the circumstances surrounding you or your life.

"You must take personal responsibility. You can not change the circumstances, the seasons, or the wind, but you can change yourself." – Jim Rohn-

J'Lynn couldn't change her past, so instead of towing it with her forever she used her past to make her life better, and to better the lives of those she encounters. She took personal responsibility for her own life. Instead of blaming her parents, blaming her family, or complaining about her past circumstances (all of which she had no control over and couldn't change), she instead acknowledged what she could control, herself, and she let go of that heavy load she had been towing. J'Lynn courageously looked inside that storage trailer, took out and faced every single thing she had placed in it. She made each trial, trauma, pain, and heartbreak become a stepping stone to the life she wanted.

"To achieve major success in life – to achieve those things that are most important to you – you must assume 100% responsibility for your life. Nothing less will do." – Jack Canfield-

In simply knowing J'lynn, she's helped build my faith that women can, do, and will continue to benefit humanity, just by being women; the strong, creative, and extraordinary women that God created us to be.

THE WOMAN'S GARDEN

Poem by Tori Vigil

As a child a man she called father planted a seed into the garden of her heart.

As a teenager a woman she called mother planted another.

She went through life's trials and through life's joys, sowing

seeds every day in her every little way. As a woman she was

hurt by a man who took and then walked away; leaving only

more seeds sown so very deep. She would catch herself in pain,

tears would flow, bad dreams would come and sometimes she

couldn't explain. One day the woman looked within and found

the seeds had grown; a garden in full bloom is what she found.

She saw beauty beyond her wildest dreams; she smelled sweet

perfume, sweeter than anything she'd ever known. But she

also saw thorns and weeds, a darkness that was trying to up-

root the beauty of her private garden. But Christ appeared in

all his glory, he took her by the hand and together they re-

moved the thorns and weeds. She cried out in pain again and

again. The roots were deep and the weeds were many, but

with each one the Lord removed she could feel the pain go too.

Each root a dream lost from shame, each weed a word care-

lessly spoken out of fear or blame, each thorn a pain inflicted

that she had not let go of. And when the deed, though hard, was done, the woman rose and found she'd changed. She was now a lady, clean, pure and redeemed. She felt consumed with love and joy and peace, at last she knew she felt complete. Now the woman sees a rainbow in the garden of her heart and she guards its gates with tender watchful care. Always watchful of who enters, always watchful of who sows seeds there......

Proverbs 4:20

"Watch over your heart with all diligence,

for out of it flow the issues of life."

"Declare today and everyday, that you are blessed with a great family, good health, faith, favor, and fulfillment. You are blessed with success, supernatural strength, and divine protection over every member of your family which God has joined together." –J'Lynn-

Now, as an ordained minister J'Lynn has answered the call on her life to build up women of faith. However, she believes that you don't have to preach from a pulpit to answer the call, but simply live a genuine Christian life everyday. This is the new Woman Leader. Over the years we've fallen into the lie that women should be considered the same as men. Yes, women should get equal pay for equal work. Yes, woman can do the same jobs that men can do. Yes, women are just as capable as men. Yes, women are equal to men, but we are not the same as men. All these things are only outward appearances, outward works. Science will confirm that we are just made differently; we think differently, we primarily use different sides of our brain than men do. Women are unique; and women should, and are embracing that uniqueness as a gift. Woman all over our great country, and all around the world are achieving success because they are women, rather than in spite of that fact. Rather than focusing on trying to be like a man they simply are themselves to the best of their ability. When you do that, you are expressing a part of who God is in you, and that kind of life is destined to achieve success.

"The day will come when man will recognize woman as his peer, not only at the fireside, but in councils of the nation. Then, and not until then, will there be the perfect comradeship, the ideal union between the sexes that shall result in the highest development of the race." –Susan B. Anthony-

The most successful preachers today whether they are male or female, are those who don't just tell you how to live your life from the pulpit. They are the ones who show you how they live their lives outside of the church building. They are successful because people learn better by seeing, by example. That's why I chose to focus on J'Lynn's leadership qualities for this book. I believe women leaders are needed at this time for the growth of humanity. I know that women have within them the God given drive to lead businesses, communities, churches, non-profits, government, and families. The stories in the bible are proof positive how women have been leaders in these areas for centuries.

You, as a reader may not aspire to be in a public place of leadership but you are probably already in a place of influence. No matter how small you may think your influence is, it is still powerful. You have the power to touch one life at a time; the life of your spouse, your children, your extended family members, your friends, the stranger at the supermarket. And who's to say what influence that person will have in the future. With one small and seemingly insignificant act you may have inadvertently influenced countless people. That is how change happens, that is how growth throughout humanity is catapulted. That is how women lead, and have been leading throughout the centuries, it's just that no one ever called it leadership.

The women leaders of the past simply did what needed to be done, brought about the results to achieve a common goal, pushed past the struggles; and perhaps it wasn't always rewarded, or valued in the way we would value our leaders of to-day, but it was leadership. Women bring a broader view of the world, add diversity of opinions, and skills; not only in the workplace, but to government, and families. The best preachers, teachers, mentors, and leaders today are those who live what they preach; teach what they know, and stand up for what they believe in. Every woman can lead in her own life, in her own way.

A SERMON WE'D LIKE TO HEAR -Poem, Author unknown

I'd rather see a sermon than hear one any day; I'd rather one should walk with me than merely show the way. The eye's a better pupil and more willing than the ear, fine counsel is confusing but examples always clear. The best of all the preachers are the one's who live their creeds, for to see God put in action is what everybody needs. I soon can learn to do it if you'll let me see it done; I can watch your hands in action, but your tongue to fast may run. The lecture you deliver may be very wise and true, but I'd rather get my lesson by observing what you do. For I might misunderstand you and the high advice you give, but there's no misunderstanding how you act and how you live. When I see a deed of kindness, I am eager to be kind. When a weaker brother stumbles and a strong man stands behind, just to see if he can help him, then the wish grows strong in me to become as big and thoughtful as I know that friend to be. All the travelers can witness that the best of guides today is not the one who tells them, but the one who shows the way. One good person teaches many, people believe what they behold; one deed of kindness noticed is worth twenty they are told. They who stand with people of honor learn to hold their honor dear, for right thinking is a language which to anyone is clear. Though an able speaker charms us with their eloquence, I say, I'd rather see a sermon then hear one any day.

J'Lynn attributes all her success in business and in her personal life to God's grace and her way of thinking. She is a positive and outgoing individual who says that to get somewhere in life you must have a vision of where you want to go, and have gratitude for where you are right now. Give thanks for what God has given you; and the people he's put in your life.

"Having a mentor is having a brain to pick, an ear to listen, and a push in the Right direction" –John Crosby-

J'Lynn has had mentors over the years who have guided her and shared with her their knowledge and experience. It's important that once you know what you want to do, find someone else who is successful at it already and glean from their years of experience. Whether it's being a great mother, a loving wife, a business woman, an artist, or whatever you have an interest in. Finding a mentor isn't that hard really. Simply ask them, you'll find more often than not that people love to help others. For some people it's hard to say "would you be my mentor", or "I think I can learn a lot from you", but having been on the receiving end of those words I can tell you that it means a lot to hear someone say them to you.

"It's important to immediately find out the key elements that make people successful. It's a lot better than wasting years making your own mistakes and learning from them the hard way."-Denise Lones-

Personal Notes

_____

_____

_____

_____

_____

_____

_____

_____

_____

_____

_____

_____

_____

Chapter Four

Brandie Seifert

Experiencing God in the broken places

Acts 26:16 But rise and stand on your feet; for I have ap-

peared to you for this purpose, to make you a minister and a

witness both of the things which you have seen and the things

which I will yet reveal to you.

Photo courtesy of Brandie Seifert

"You know there is really a God

When you experience his love in your broken places"

-Brandie Seifert-

A CROWN OF PURPOSE

Many of us associate our most deeply-held convictions with a single, and often life-changing experience. Others have always held certain beliefs sacred. In either case, it is important to talk about our experience and share our story with others. Brandie struggled to tell her story, and reveal the secrets of her past. She often felt ashamed, embarrassed, and worried that others would see her as someone to feel sorry for, but she longed to help others who had been through similar traumas. Brandie found her voice, her platform, and her courage to follow that dream of helping others when she became Mrs. Texas and had a crown placed on her head.

Many pageant queens are bringing their moral convictions and life experiences into the pageant industry and making a huge difference. If you are a light in an already bright place then you don't have much of an impact, but if you are a light in a dark place then you can cause change. With the pressure to be thin and the focus on outer beauty it's tempting to conform to what the typical pageant industry is looking for; especially if you are a young woman or a first time pageant queen. Yet, making a conscious choice to remain true to herself and hold strong to her morals, has already proven successful for Brandie Seifert, and many other reigning queens who are choosing to view their crown as an opportunity to pursue their purpose in life.

Like Brandie, many in pageantry have chosen to let creativity shine; to step out of the box; break out of the mold, and stand out from society at large. Many pageants today require their queens to choose a platform, and for some pageant partici-pants, choosing a platform is just another step in the pageant process, but for others, like Brandie, it is an extension of their life's work to be a light in a dark place. Some amazing, and compassionate queens are allowing their platforms to take them into prisons, hospitals, homeless shelters, schools, and foster homes. Other platforms are taking queens in front of the media where they are shining the light on serious issues such as: child abuse, eating disorders, poverty, and teen pregnancy.

To Brandie a crown of purpose involved more than being a queen for mere outward appearance, having a title, or wearing a crown because of the need for attention, or validation. A crown of purpose is the choice to step into the spotlight, not for you, but for others. Ambrose Redmoon said, "Courage is not the absence of fear, but rather the judgment that something else is more important than fear." Courage and fears come in many forms and sometimes it takes courage just to be ourselves, to look in the mirror everyday and say I am beautiful without makeup, I am enough without any titles or crowns. I am powerful because my strength comes from within. I am a warrior because I can fight for change that will better the future for all women.

There are a large percentage of women participating in pageants today who have survived: cancer, child abuse, domestic violence, rape, sexual abuse, and other traumas. Looking at these beautiful women you'd probably never guess that they've ever experienced any kind of trauma, but it is nothing to be ashamed of, and definitely not something that should be swept under a rug. It makes sense that we're seeing more and more queens taking advantage of their reign and coming forward with courage to talk about their survival, and their healing process; because they have a strong desire to help others become survivors instead of remaining victims. It is healing to creatively express your pain in a positive way. Many survivors around the world are choosing creative expression as a form of healing. It's only natural that this message has come into the pageant world. Many queens believe that having a crown helps others to view their survival story as a positive one, rather than being seen as someone to feel sorry for they are viewed as strong women for their ability to overcome adversity and turn it into something positive. There are even some queens who have founded non-profits because of their experiences and they are changing the world one life at a time.

A big applaud should go out to these women for taking a stand, making their convictions known and letting their voices be heard. There are deep wounds etched within a child after they have been touched by a life of abuse. Wounds cause many thoughts and those thoughts lead to many emotions, emotions of shame, guilt, anger, resentment and fear. All of which even they themselves may be unaware of. When in their eyes the world has neglected them they trust no one and begin to loose hope, but there is a God who can look into their soul and heal the broken places he finds there. God reveals to them that they are not an accident, He created them on purpose and for a purpose. There is a power that is able to touch those broken places and make that child or grown woman, as the case may be, and make them whole again. The power that heals is the power of love, namely God's perfect and unfailing love.

Brandie's Story

After what seemed like the perfect day, Brandie looked out at the amazing sunset, and mulled over the many activities that were playing back in her mind. It was her first experience at a summer camp, but more importantly it was also her first experience with God. She was thinking about how her life would be different now, and maybe somehow it would be better. Now that she had asked Jesus into her life.

Though that is a significant act for anyone at any age, for fifteen year old Brandie it was a miracle in itself that she even made it to that Christian summer camp. She had endured thirteen years of living in horrible conditions; surrounded by drug use; experiencing physical, and sexual abuse from her mother, father and occasionally other family members; moving from place to place; and being in foster care. She had finally found a friend who invited her along to camp for the summer. This was the beginning of a journey with Christ, a journey of love that brought healing from a broken past. This was the first time Brandie experienced God in the middle of her broken life.

For someone who's never experienced abuse it might be diffi-cult to understand the brokenness you can feel, but if you have experienced it, you know that it leaves deep wounds that seem to never heal. For Brandie, it was faith in Christ that brought healing into her life and the strength she needed to endure the healing process. Though Brandie endured a five year healing process she says that it was well worth the effort and gives us a quote from one of her favorite authors.

"It's better to feel the pain now, rather than live in it forever"

–Joyce Meyer-

For Brandie, and for myself, healing is a continual process. As with anyone who has been abused, there are still issues from time to time that pop up in our lives, and require God's loving hand. After all healing is not a one time thing, it's a process. Just like love is not a one time thing, it must be cared for so it can grow, and be sustained. Brandie wanted her family, and friends to be able to say that the driving force in her life is her love for God and not her pain from the past.

Pain, whether emotional or physical leaves a broken place, fear often is the first thing that will come and try to fill that broken place. However, when Gods love is your driving force then it's his love that fills those broken places and allows you to accomplish anything, because you are in Gods hands. Love makes relationships become your highest priority. Love makes your life moldable, love helps you to be changeable, and love helps you to easily adapt. Love conquers all, especially when it's God's unconditional, Agape love.

Jeremiah

"Like clay in the hand of the potter, so are you in my hand"

Brandie is grateful for having Christ in her life. She wants to make a difference for others who have been abused, and now have broken places in their heart, and lives. "It's a shame that a success story like mine is the exception" she said. For most abused children the cycle is never broken. They grow up to become abusers themselves or they marry abusers, and live their lives in fear on a daily basis. The sad truth is that most turn to drug use or sexual promiscuity trying to escape the pain.

"I believe things happen for a reason, and even when bad things happen God is not to blame. He gives us free will, and he has shown me that he was hurting right along with me."

–Brandie–

Life here on earth is only a temporary thing. No matter what you believe about an after life, I think we can all agree that we will not live forever in this form. So we can either live this life stuck in the past, worried about the future, or we can enjoy the present. The past can not be changed or altered in any way, it does not exist anymore except in our memories. The past has no power except that which we imagine it has. The future has not yet come, and any choice we make now will alter the course of our future. So the present is the only thing that's real, it's the only thing we have some control over. The present is the only thing we can truly enjoy. Even if we are enjoying memories of the past we are enjoying those memories right now in the present. How you feel, and what you think in this moment is what matters most. Now, this moment is the most powerful moment in your life because it's the moment you're in. Love will be at it's most powerful when you love now. Don't wait until later to love God, to love yourself, and to love others. Later may never come.

REAL LOVE - Poem by Tori Vigil

Today I want to love...I want to give the kind of love that God gives. I want to see the kind of love that's given in many ways the eye may not notice. I want to feel the kind of love that touches the soul. I want to be the kind of love that Christ is. I want to know the kind of love that's real.

Today I want to love...The kind of love that is patient, preserv-

ing the good always. Submitting to the will of God in all things, calm and quiet in the midst of turbulence or chaos, unruffled by the noises that surround us, uncomplaining endurance through life's many circumstances and difficult decisions that come our way.

Today I want to love...The kind of love that is kindness, expressing only goodness, proving to have the character of Christ, showing the gentleness of heaven, reaching out with a tender touch and a gentle word; acting from unselfish motives, the kind of love that causes us to become the very mercy of God.

Today I want to love...The kind of love that refuses to step into jealousy, never envious but thankful, never boastful but bold, never proud but humble, never haughty but meek, never rude but caring, never demanding but giving, never irritable but at peace, never touchy but tranquil, never holding a grudge but forgiving.

Today I want to love...The kind of love that rejoices in the truth, that is loyal, that always expects the best, that is perfect, that casts out all fears, and that endures forever.

Today I want to love...The kind of love that is ever moving forward, always challenging, forever deepening, continually growing stronger, and day by day multiplying to those around me...

Today I want to love for the sake of love itself...

Brandie now age 29, is a professional make-up artist featured with numerous prestigious lines. She works in production and film including an award winning Emmy TV Show, as well as for various other television productions. She also freelances for many fashion shows, and Model shoots. She travels all over the city of Houston, and often times to other parts of the country to do her work. Brandie believes strongly that make-up only enhances a woman on the outside, what makes her beautiful is what's on the inside.

Brandie loves the fact that she can see a woman walk away feeling completely beautiful, but she admits at times it can be difficult. Women are their own worst critics and everyone has flaws they want to cover up, and hide from the world. At times it can be difficult to assure a woman she looks beautiful no matter what brand or color of makeup she is wearing.

If women could simply see their inner beauty and let that shine through they'd be much happier. Other people are drawn to those who believe in themselves. That belief, and confidence in who God created her to be, and what her purpose in life is lead her to be crowned "Mrs. Texas Outstanding Woman in America" in 2007. I happened to be there at the moment when it was announced that she had won, and I saw her face as they placed the crown on her head. She took the opportunity the universe had given her, and used her platform to really make a difference in the lives of abused children. She truly is a beautiful person inside and out. Every great accomplishment that people have been able to achieve has been a result of them overcoming guilt and fear. Fear is the main emotion that blocks success.

"The ability to face fear is the key to unlimited success...you must remember that fear is a conditioned belief. You were not born with fear, you learned how to be afraid." – Joe Nunziata-

What is fear really? I heard someone say once, fear is :

False

Evidence that

Appears

Real

I did a lot of research about fear when I was getting ready to talk about it on my radio show in the episode titled "Facing Your Fears." I came to realize that fear is an emotional state, and like all of our emotions it has an affect on the entire body. When you fear something, whether the fear is real or imagined, your body makes it real; because you feel it emotionally, and mentally. I often refer to this reaction as "a deer in the headlights." If you've ever driven at night through the woods, and had a deer run across the road in front of you, then you know what I mean. It's not that they are foolish creatures. They know there is danger when they see the headlights coming toward them, but their body becomes so consumed with fear they can't move their muscles. The fear paralyzes them. Often the result of not moving gets them hit by the passing vehicle, and results in their untimely death. Which of course not only affects that deer, but it's family, the driver of the vehicle, anyone else in the vehicle, their families, and the car. Fear has a ripple affect, much like anger, or any other powerful emotion. It's results are an energy that ripples through time and space, and affects others in your life.

Often you will play a fearful scenario in your head over, and over again; fearing the result of a decision, or an upcoming circumstance. Had you not been afraid then whatever the decision, or circumstance might have been you would have only experienced it once, while in that moment, but fear made you experience it over and over again, often before anything ever happened. When the decision was made or the circumstance finally happened it probably wasn't as bad as you thought it would be.

"Cowards die many times before their deaths.

The valiant never taste of death but once" –Shakespeare-

The most common fear people experience is the fear of failure, and the fear of success. Fear of failure will be defined differently by different people. Everyone defines failure according to their own view of the world. One person may say failure to them is not achieving their goals in a certain time frame, while another person may say failure is not having an income of over

$100,000 a year; yet someone else may say failure is not having an income of over a million dollars a year. You are not a failure or a success because someone else says you are; you are a failure or a success because you think you are. You define your own life according to your beliefs and values.

Question 1:

1. What does it mean for you to be a success?

2. What does it mean for you to be a failure?

3. Who or what helped you define the answers to question 1 & 2? (if it was your past, your parents, or anything outside yourself then now is the time to redefine your success and failures in life).

My answers to questions:

1. What does it mean for you to be a success: "I am a success if I give my best in whatever it is I do, and if I learn something."

2. What does it mean for you to be a failure: "I can't fail even if I didn't give my best I can still learn something from it... I am not a failure."

Having defined my success and failure for myself, the only way I can fail is if I never learn anything from a decision, circumstance, or mistake. Make two new definitions now about what will make you a success and failure, define them for yourself from within yourself based on your values and beliefs. What would you do with your life if you knew you couldn't fail? Make it easy for yourself to succeed and hard to fail.

Brandie has determined her own beliefs and values and takes actions in her life to support those beliefs and values, that's how you become successful. Brandie values being the wife to her husband, Ryan Seiffert. She values how beautiful women are, and she values children. That is why she works with several organizations that reach out, and speak up on behalf of abused children, and children in the foster care system; organizations such as the "Child Advocates of Fort bend" and "A Helping Hand for Healing Souls." Whether anyone else may think so or not Brandie is successful because she thinks she is. Define for yourself what it means to be a success and what it means to be a failure.

"Hearing about others abused lives can be gut wrenching, but it has given me even more compassion."-Brandie-

According to the "Texas Council on Family Violence", violence against children effects their physical health, it affects their emotional well being, their behavior, and their social skills; all of which will continue into adulthood if not dealt with. Each child reacts to violence in different ways according to their age group. For instance infants may have frequent illness, difficulty sleeping, and developmental delays. Preschool children may become regressive, irritable, and fearful of being alone. Elementary age children might become hostile because they need to externalize their problems; whereas adolescents might resort to drugs, sexual acting out, and running away from home.

Stop abuse! Don't be an abuser and don't be abused...

The types of abuse are:

- Physical Abuse (hitting, throwing things, choking, threats against your life, pointing a gun, knife or other weapon, etc.)

- Verbal & mental (insults, cursing, tearing people down, threatening to kill themselves or others)

- Sexual (rape, incest, unwanted touching, vulgar comments)

Warning signs of an abuser are:

Below is a list of common abusive behaviors to watch for:

- Criticism about your good qualities

- Past abusive relationships

- Criminal activities

- Drinking or drug problems, past or present

- Mood swings

- Discourages your successes

- They are very jealous and possessive

- Has abusive family members or spouses or siblings

- Attempts to control your whereabouts

- Disrespect toward you or your family members publicly or privately

- Violations of others rights

- Irresponsibility

- Attempts to keep you isolated, and keep you away from friends and family

- Persistent lying

- History of truancy, delinquency and running away

- Highly reactive

- Streaks of meanness toward others for no reason

- Calls you names and humiliates you or others

- Threatened by relationships with men, past, present or imagined

- Abusive to animals

- Controlling

- Insults you about how you look, act, or choices you make

How to report abuse or get help:

Many people aren't sure if child abuse, or domestic violence is an area where they should get involved in. Especially if they aren't sure if the child is really being abused; how severe the abuse is, or if they aren't really sure if it is domestic violence. It's always better to error on the side of over reporting, error on the side of caution. Abuse is unacceptable no matter how severe. Keep in mind that most children who are being abused can't speak up for themselves and need an adult to stand up for them. Often times they are so used to the abuse that they don't even know it's wrong. They don't know that life can be any different.

- Call the police

- Call child services

- Call a hotline that helps women and children

If you are being abused:

- Talk to a counselor

- Reach out to family and friends

- Call one of the many hotlines that help abused women & children (see back of book)

- Get out of an unsafe environment as quickly as possible

It is not easy to seek help, I've spoken with many women in abusive relationships who all experience the same fears. As said earlier fear is what keeps people small, fear is what the abuser relies on to bring about compliance. You have to see safety, value safety, need safety more than you've come to need that abuser. Women often tolerate the abuse because they see their tolerance as the only way to be safe. "He just needs to get it out of his system then we'll be ok", is what I've often heard. It is a dangerous cycle. The calm after the storm, and before the next is not safety it is an opportunity to seek change. Abused women must seek that change with all the passion for life they have left in them.

It's not until they've gotten out of the unsafe and abusive environment that they can see how trapped and limited they really were. It's then when they find out how beautiful and talented they are. That's the beauty of hindsight. That's the freedom from fear. A woman who can overcome abuse like that can overcome anything life brings her way.

Personal Notes

_____

_____

_____

_____

_____

_____

_____

_____

_____

_____

_____

_____

_____

_____

Chapter Five

Susan Wolf

The power of Gratitude and Positive thinking

"An attitude of gratitude cultivates

a harvest of happiness and joy"

By Tori Vigil

Photo courtesy of Susan Wolf

"Expressing Gratitude is a form of Love"

-Susan Wolf-

I used to think that I must have been absent the day God handed out humor to everyone, perhaps you can relate. Has anyone ever told you to loosen up, lighten up, live a little, have some fun? I've heard that a lot. I've never really thought of myself as having a sense of humor, and I seemed to have lost the art of just being playful when I grew up. I am used to being thought of as the sensible, and serious one in my family, much like Susan Wolf. But when I met Susan she brought humor back into my life.

I first met Susan at the event for Outstanding Women in America, and I got a glimpse of her playfulness. I remember thinking I wish I could be that playful, and not care what anyone thinks. As I got to know her more she is a serious person, but there seems to be a balance in her life. I guess I just always assumed that fun people were super hyper all the time, and serious people were super serious all the time. Well never assume anything in life.

Susan's gratefulness for the little things, and her positive attitude about things in general just made it nice to be around her. Have you ever met anyone like that? Enjoy their presence in your life because they are a gift. I gradually began to think about humor, laughter, happiness, and joy, like I think about creativity. All those things are a part of who God is, and therefore I have access to them whenever I need them. God did give me a sense of humor...

THE STATE OF HAPPINESS

Is happiness something only a few are blessed with, a state of being, or a destination we may someday get to if...?

Actually most of the great philosophers, teachers, and spiritual beings of the past say that happiness is a choice. Happiness is a part of the journey of life rather than a destination we will get to someday. What I've learned over the years is that no one, and nothing can make you happy. Not all the money in the world, not all the crowns, or jewels, or any title that people can bestow on you. The richest people in the world still commit suicide, yet the poorest people in the world can be the most fulfilled with life such as Mother Theresa.

The choice to be happy is yours and yours alone. So if the choice is yours, and it is, why not be happy? You deserve happiness. It's when you find yourself in that state of happiness, with that inner joy, that life just seems more fun, and the whole world seems to be on your side. Happiness really is when you are "at one with the universe", or "at peace with who you are" no matter what life may throw at you. Gandhi said that "happiness is when what you think, what you say, and what you do are all in harmony." When your life is in harmony, that is a high energy level to be at, and you attract other things and people into your life who are also vibrating at that high energy level.

Have you ever notice that when a person comes to the end of their life they never look back and say they wished they had made more money, or that they wished they had worked harder, longer hours at their job. If only they had gotten that bigger house, or bought that more expensive car. They look back at the things, and relationships which mattered most to them. They wish they had put more time and energy into those things, and into those relationships. Goethe once said that "things which matter most should never be at the mercy of things which matter least." Yet that is what most of us do our entire lives, sometimes never noticing it until it's too late. When the things which matter most are in their rightful place in your life, then everything else just falls into its rightful place. You'll then find your life to be more harmonious, happier, and more fulfilling then you ever thought possible.

It's not to say that you shouldn't have things or want things. I believe the universe wants to bless us, because God wants to bless us. We just need to be open to see those blessing/gifts when they come our way, then be able to enjoy and appreciate them. We need to choose to receive them, and be grateful. How often do you hear people say, "Oh I couldn't possibly accept that gift," or "you shouldn't have done that". Have you said those things yourself? Life is full of gifts God wants to bless us with every day. By responding to the universe in such a way you deprive God, and others of the joys to be found in giving. To help you reach your state of happiness make time daily to reflect on the things that matter most, pray, and be positive. Bellow you will find the optimists creed read it daily if you need to. Choose daily to be happy, you deserve it.

The optimists Creed

I Promise myself:

To be so strong that nothing can disturb my peace of mind.

To talk health, happiness, and prosperity to every person I meet.

To make all my friends feel that there is something worthwhile in them.

To look at the sunny side of everything

and make my optimism come true.

To think only of the best, to work only for the best

and to expect only the best.

To be just as enthusiastic about the success of others

as I am about my own.

To forget the mistakes of the past

and press on to the greater achievements of the future.

To wear a cheerful expression at all times,

and give a smile to every living creature I meet.

To give so much time to improving myself that I have no time to

criticize others.

To be too large for worry, too noble for anger, too strong for

fear,

and too happy to permit the presence of trouble.

To think well of myself and to proclaim this fact to the world,

not in loud word, but in great deeds.

To live in the faith that the whole world is on my side,

so long as I am true to the best that is in me.

The Power of Gratitude

Standing center stage, eyes tearing, staring out at the crowd, everyone is looking at you, and the crown is being placed on your head. You experience a myriad of emotions in that moment; happiness, joy, and most of all gratitude. Gratitude is a powerful emotion that produces an abundance of energy. Gratitude also frees up your creative abilities and allows you more freedom to tap into new ideas.

-CICERO-

"Gratitude is not only the greatest of virtues,

but the parent of all the others"

In a 1998 Gallup poll, the majority of Americans said they express gratitude toward God (54%) and gratitude toward others (67%). What that means is that 33% of the time we either aren't grateful, or don't show it. These numbers only account for gratitude toward things we think are good. Although gratitude is something anyone can experience; those who are grateful more often are also happier, more forgiving, less depressed, and sick less often. Those people say they express gratitude even for the not so good circumstances in life.

"Happiness cannot be traveled to, owned, earned, worn or consumed. Happiness is the spiritual experience of living every minute

with love, grace and gratitude." –Denis Waitley-

Gratitude on an individual level says you are grateful for a crown, a title, a house, a marriage, children and the things we currently have or have been given in the past, which is great. Now, how about taking gratitude to the next level? Gratitude on a universal level says you are grateful for life, love, freedoms, time, space, others, ideas, concepts, your ego, hardships and blessings. It's not necessarily something you have to concentrate on continually, once you allow it to become part of your underlying thoughts, this happens over time. This type of gratitude is not connected to circumstances because it is a choice. You are choosing to be grateful for your life no matter what the circumstance may seem like at any given moment. You can be grateful for not winning a crown because the contest drew out the best in you, perhaps you learned something new about yourself, gained a new friend, and it was the experience itself that has added to your life.

"Gratitude unlocks the fullness of life. It turns what we have into enough, and more. It turns denial into acceptance, chaos into order, and confusion into clarity.... It turns problems into gifts, failures into success, the unexpected into perfect timing, and mistakes into important events. Gratitude makes sense of our past, brings peace for today and creates a vision for tomorrow." –Melodie Beattie-

Eventually gratitude will cease being something you do, and it will become a part of who you are. You stop saying "I am grateful for--" and you just say "I am grateful". It may be a process. You may have to start with small things. Try making a list of things to be grateful for, choose something you wouldn't normally consider having gratitude for. Be grateful for breathing, music, your biggest failures, your weaknesses. Think of gratitude as a magnifying glass that allows you to see something good you couldn't see before about that situation or experience. You are then magnifying the good, concentrating on the good and in turn attracting more good things to you. I can say from personal experience that this is true. When life ceased being something I needed to win and I simply magnified what I believed, life took on a whole new meaning and began to go in the direction I'd always dreamed of.

-RABBI HAROLD KUSHNER-

"If you concentrate on finding whatever is good in every situation, you will discover that your life will suddenly be filled with gratitude, a feeling that nurtures the soul."

So what does gratitude have to do with success? Gratitude is a necessity for a successful life. In a world so consumed by instant gratification and instant results, it's harder to stay focused on the things that really matter. A conscious effort to remain grateful, even for the small things, causes you to also remain focused. It's easy to be caught up with the issues of the ego, like pride, boastfulness, greed, and so on.

A successful woman transcends her own needs, and sees the needs of those around her. She then sets a plan in motion to provide for those needs. A successful leader does even more than that, and inspires others to do the same. Today's woman leaders inspire others to greatness, and success far beyond what they dreamed possible for themselves.

A grateful woman is a confidant woman. If you are grateful for your story, then you believe in yourself. If you don't believe in yourself, not very many others are going to believe in you either. Confidence is beautiful, and it draws people to you. People like to be around people who believe in themselves. In a sense you teach others how to treat you by how you treat yourself. Self confidence isn't prideful; rather it's assurance in your beliefs, values, skills, abilities, moral character, and the person God made you to be.

As I've mentored and counseled many young women, I've found that one of the main things they lack on their journey to success is confidence. Why is it that so many women lack confidence? Was it the way they were raised, the lack of knowledge, lack of education? I say no, it's not any of these things. Though these things can contribute to a lack of confidence they aren't the source. Again, I believe that it's fear. Fear of the unknown.

When you enter into any circumstance no matter what it might be, or what area of your life it pertains to. If you are unsure of the outcome then you are doubtful of your abilities to achieve the desired result. That leads to fear of failure and a lack of confidence. So how do you overcome that? Hope & expectation! The bible says that hope is the assurance of things not yet seen. So go into any situation expecting something good to happen. You don't have to be perfect, or have all the answers, you aren't responsible to fix all the problems in the universe. If you carry that weight around, then of course it's hard to be confident. Just believe in yourself. Be true to who you are.

"The universe will correspond to nature of your song"

-Rev. Michael Beckwith-

I've heard people say we'll I am just a shy person, it's just not in my nature to be outgoing and confident. People are not born shy, they learn to be shy. Therefore you can learn to be confident. Susan Wolf shared that shyness and insecurity were her childhood companions, and they attempted to follow her into adulthood. She gave her life to GOD, and with his help overcame much of that shyness and insecurity. Like me, she learned that the joy of the Lord is our strength. We can do all things through CHRIST who strengthens us.

Actually you were born confident. As a child you were totally confident in what you wanted. If you wanted food, to be changed, or to be held you vocalized that want and desire with confidence. You could also use the word faith. You were confident, and had faith that once you expressed what you wanted that need would be met. If you had decent care takers that need was met. Over the years someone told you "no you can't have that", "no don't touch that", "you can't have everything you want", and so on. All of that may have jilted your confidence or even shattered it.

Well ok, so maybe in the past you didn't get the things you wanted. Maybe you were shy, maybe you did lack confidence, but that is not who you have to be now. This is where gratitude comes in. Whatever you experienced in your past, not matter how much you think you failed, it didn't kill you. What doesn't kill you makes you stronger. Of all the possible outcomes that could come about because of your failure to get desired results, death would be the worst. Well since that didn't happen then what is left to fear, but fear itself.

"Experience is what you get when you didn't get what you wanted" –unknown-

You always get something, so choose to be grateful for what you did get, the chance to do things differently next time. Be grateful that you've learned from the experience, and learning was the successful outcome. If you know you can have success in every situation in life by choosing to be grateful and learn from every situation your confidence/faith begins to grow.

Take for instance a guitar student. When they first begin to practice they complain that it hurts their finger tips, they aren't immediately getting the results they want; some of them give up. Those who press on past the experience of practice and blistered hands, learn to play well, even beautifully. Their confidence grows, and eventually they become proficient with their instrument. Confidence may take time to grow but it's worth the effort.

Here are some easy steps to take to build your confidence when you need it in a hurry:

1. Stop what you're doing or thinking about, and do something different; stretch, stand up, smile or anything else you can think of. This breaks the pattern of thinking that's contributing to your lack of confidence.

2. Act confident, stand or sit up straight and tall; think of a happy memory; remember your greatest accomplishments and achievements. This changes your mood to a more affirming and positive one.

3. Focus on the desired result, picture things going the way you want them to; allow yourself to feel right in the moment the joy and excitement of what it will be like to have your desired results; Express that joy in some way,

such as clap your hands, shout a whoop, my favorite is to do a happy dance. If others are around you it will make them smile too, or if it's not in an appropriate place, snap your fingers, or something else discreet. You'll find that when you focus on positive results you in turn become positive.

Just try these things, and see if after you've done them, if you are still in the same state of mind you were before you did them. It's impossible to stay doubtful, fearful, and sad when you change your focus.

Going back to that confident child who knew exactly what she wanted, do you still know what you want? Do you have a vision for your life, career, and family? I don't know if you've ever seen the movie "Alice in Wonderland", but there is a scene where Alice asks the Cheshire cat which way she should go. The cat told her it depends on where she wants to go. When she told the cat it didn't matter, he in turn told her then it didn't matter which way she went. This is how most of us go through life. Not knowing or caring where our life is heading. Of course it's hard to be grateful for anything if we refuse to acknowledge anything that's happened, is happening or will happen in our life due to a lack of vision.

-Proverbs 29:18 -

"Where there is no vision the people (perish) are unrestrained"

The bible tells us that where there is a lack of vision the people perish. Vision is mentioned 73 times in the King James Version of the Bible. Every successful person I've talked to has a vision for their life, they gave set goals based on what they believe is their major purpose in life. So what exactly is a vision? Put simply a vision is a detailed yet brief description of what you want and where you want to be. About two years ago I really sat down and reevaluated my life. In doing so I was able to create and define my vision. I decided what it was I wanted for myself and for humanity. After creating my vision I could then make goals in line with that vision. Goals give you direction, they help you take steps; actions; and make decisions daily, weekly, monthly, and yearly to get closer to making your vision a reality. When you have a clear vision you can then set up a plan of action to accomplish your vision. Without question you should write down your vision and goals.

–BRIAN TRACY-

"Decide upon your major definite purpose in life
And then organize all your activities around it."

Bill Gates Vision:

"To put a computer on every desktop and in every home"

President JFK's Vision:

"To put a man on the moon by the end of the decade"

Walt Disney's Vision:

"to create a place where parents and children could have fun together."

By Tori Vigil

Tori's vision:

"To inspire women of all ages to live creatively, define their own womanhood, and embrace their destiny."

Susan's vision:

"To combine ministry with entertainment, and filming for the purpose of evangelism, and teaching Godly concepts."

"If you can effectively articulate your vision and create excitement that makes people passionate, there is no limit to what you can achieve." - Mike Olexa-

Susan's Story

Susan is a wife and mother of two grown children. She is listed as an associate member of the Mississippi Christian Entertain-

155

ers, and she is a member of the Gulf Coast Film/TV and Music Industry. She's filmed a 15 week class for Kingdom Works International (http://kingdom-works.com/ , 4502 Shortcut Road, Pascagoula, MS) that teaches the various perspectives of crossing cultural barriers in missions, including God's perspective. Susan also founded her own organization: The Gulf Coast Christian Entertainers, and Filmmakers Association. She most recently finished directing and producing a film project titled "The Holy Cow MOOvie". After overcoming years of alcoholism, Susan wanted to leave a legacy that would speak to generations to come, and she chose to do that through film.

It wasn't easy admitting to, and overcoming a problem with alcohol that started as high school rebellion. In college, that simple high school rebellion got progressively worse as did her drinking. Susan shared with me that "it started as just something to do with friends, but I was unaware that I was gradually growing dependent on the alcohol." Granted Susan didn't fit the stereotype of a typical alcoholic. After all, almost every adult drinks, right? It's socially acceptable to drink when you're an adult. Most people think that you're either an alcoholic or your not; either you have a drinking problem or you don't. So though Susan didn't drink often, when she did drink, she did so heavily.

The alcohol had been keeping Susan in a state of deep depression, because she had begun to use it as a crutch to escape her emotions. Her turning point came one morning, when she knew she couldn't function as a mom in her hung-over state. She was watching the Christian channel, when a man came on with the message Susan needed to hear. "You can't overcome the problems/addictions in your life until you put your foot down, and determine you don't want them anymore."

Does Susan's story sound familiar? It does to me; it reminds me of the story told in the bible of the prodigal son. His clothes drenched with the smell of a pig pen, his head down turned as he drudged down the familiar path to his father's house. His thoughts were focused on regretting the past, and dreading the future. The last year of his life had been a rollercoaster ride of parties, women, and the lifestyle of a drug addicted rock star. "What will I say to him, he probably hates me, why should he let me come home, I'm such a disappointment" he thought to himself as he rehashed what he was going to say to his father. He was so focused on his self pity, and fear that he didn't even notice the sound of his father's shouts as he ran towards him. He was shocked out of his numbed state by his father's strong embrace.

God is like the prodigal son's father. No matter what we've done, or said, or how badly we've behaved, God is waiting for us to return to him. He's waiting with open arms, longing to celebrate our home coming. Just as God delighted in Susan's decision to let go of her poor choices and seek Him; God will also delight in your choice seek after him with all your heart. (See Luke chapter 15)

So why all the rebellion, why the drinking? For the same reason we all do the things we do that are not in line with God's will. We do those things because we're seeking something, trying to fill that emptiness, trying to quench that thirst. No matter what it is you are using to fill that hole or quench that thirst, only God can bring us relief, healing, and a new life.

Using drugs? It may numb the pain for awhile, but drugs can't numb your emotions or your thoughts forever; and they can't heal your soul. Spending money? It can buy you things you want, supply you with what you need to survive, but it can't buy what your spirit needs. Seeking sex? It can feel good for awhile, but it can't replace the human need to give, and receive real love. Got religion? The good deeds can pacify us, but never really satisfy us. My Grandmother always used to say that sitting in a garage doesn't make you car anymore than sitting in church makes you a Christian. God desires from us a relationship that is real; a relationship where there is communication, and love daily. That kind of relationship is what helped Susan, and all the women in this book let go of their past; and embrace their future. What kind of relationship with God do you have; and are you letting God fill your emptiness and quench your thirst?

Personal Notes

_____

_____

_____

_____

_____

_____

_____

_____

_____

_____

_____

_____

_____

_____

_____

Chapter Six

Summary of how to achieve success

How can we as ordinary women achieve extraordinary success?

"Curiosity, Confidence, Courage, and Constancy.

And the greatest of these is Confidence." –Walt Disney-

The following pages consist of a list which summarizes how you can heal from your past, and achieve success. Each summary statement is accompanied by an assignment that is meant to help you focus on your potential; on being more positive, and affirming; and excel in your journey of spiritual growth.

1. Believe, be confident that you are capable of extraordinary success because that's how God made you (Psalm 119:66 NIV "Teach me knowledge and good judgment for I believe in your commands)

2. Believe, be confident in yourself, and in all the talents, gifts, and abilities God has given you (Matthew 25:15 NIV "to one he gave five talents, to another 2 talents, and to another 1 talent, each one according to his ability")

3. Give your worries, and your life over to a higher power (Matthew 11:28-30 NIV "Come to me, all you who are

weary and burdened, and I will give you rest. Take my yoke upon you and learn from me, for I am gentle and humble of heart, and you will find rest for your souls. For my yoke is easy and my burden is light.")

4. Trust that the Creator Of The Universe is on your side, and wants the best for you (Luke 11:10 NIV "for everyone who asks receives; he who seeks finds; and to him who knocks the door will be opened".)

5. Figure out what your gifts, talents and purpose is by doing what you love, then pursue that with all your passion, drive, and determination (Exodus 9:16 NIV "But I have raised you up for this purpose, that I might show you my power and that my name might be proclaimed in all the earth".)

6. Create a wonderful vision for yourself, and for your life (Proverbs 29:18 KJV "Where there is no vision the people perish")

7. Overcome your greatest fears. Fear is the main emotion that blocks success. "Run toward your fears there is noting to fear but fear itself" It does not glorify God to live in fear, and limit your potential (1 John 4:18 NIV "There is no fear in love. But perfect love casts out the fear.")

8. Dare to dream, and dream big, set goals in line with Gods will pertaining to your dreams, and work toward accomplishing those goals

9. Be happy all day long, everyday even if you don't feel like it. It's not that you are trying to be fake, but that you are consciously putting yourself in a better frame of mind (remember happiness is a choice not a destination)

10. Have a positive, and affirmative attitude "I can do anything", "I can be what I want to be", "I have a purpose", "I am full of hope, and faith", "I am worthy of success"

11. Define your own womanhood, and embrace your destiny, no one else can tell you who you are, or what you should be

12. If someone says you can't do something or be something, prove them wrong

13. Worship in the faith of your choice, because worship is a sign of thankfulness; appreciation; love, and gratitude

14. Everyone has within them the ability to achieve success and inspire others to do the same, access that ability and never forget it's there

15. Never pay attention to the nay-Sayers who laugh at your dreams, inwardly they really wish they had the courage to follow their own passions

16. Don't be afraid to take risks, if you follow your heart the means of accomplishing something will come to you

17. Take life one step at a time. The past no longer exists, and the future is not yet here, so enjoy the present moment

18. Touch one life at a time, that puts one trickle of hope into the pool of humanity and starts a ripple who's momentum will build, and you'll be surprised what it will do

19. Focus on all the good things in your life and in the lives of those around you

20. Surround yourself with positive people, who believe in you, and will lift you higher

21. Ask! Ask for help when you need it, ask for advice, ask for what you want, ask for support, ask for information. People can not read minds so don't be afraid to ask!

22. If you see a need, fill that need, you don't have to wait for someone else to make the changes in society you want to see

23. Be a woman of strong character; live your life with honesty, with compassion, sincerity, integrity, and vision

24. Take full responsibility for your life, and every choice you've made in it

25. Be an eternal student, read constantly, observe the world around you, life always has something to teach us (the most influential women in history loved to read)

26. Be a writer, you don't need to write a book simply keep a journal of all the things you are grateful for; all the things that make you happy, all your answered prayers. It will keep you focused on all the abundance in your life.

27. Find a mentor in the field you want to pursue and glean from their knowledge and experience

28. Don't live your life trying to please others, rather please God, he already told us how in the Bible

29. READ Gods word daily, The Bible is life's little instruction book

30. MOST IMPORTANTLY ...Pray for yourself, and Pray for others. When I go to God to ask for something, I go knowing that something I am asking for already exists. I go to God believing that what I want also wants me because God, being my father wants to bless me, and provide abundantly for me. Pray with gratitude and thankful anticipation; picturing what it will feel like, look like, sound like, be like when what I pray for arrives. True prayer is being in Gods holy presence. In His presence scarcity, lack, and doubt can not exist. (The apostle Paul often asked people to pray for him. He did so because 1. he knew prayer has power and 2. because he expected change to happen. Prayers affect lives, not just yours but the people you are praying for as well; be it family, friends, or the president)

Joshua 1:8

"Never stop reciting these words, but you shall meditate on it day and night, so that you may be careful to do according to all that is written in it; for then you will make your way prosperous, and then you will have success."

Lucille Ball was told that she was too shy to be in acting; The Beatles were told they didn't have a good sound; Michael Jordan was cut from his high school basketball team, and he went home and cried; Thomas Edison was told he was too stupid to learn anything; Abraham Lincoln lost his fiancé, filed bankruptcy, and was defeated in 8 elections. So what made all these people go on to great success?

–CHARLES KETTERING-

"Believe and act as if it's impossible to fail."

All the above mentioned people believed in themselves. Their belief, and confidence was a choice they made in spite of what they were being told, or the circumstances that surrounded them. If you've ever fallen short at anything then you are in good company, because many successful people today will tell you they have been right there with you. Whatever it was, it was not a failure. You just learned another way not to do something. Success is not about being blessed with opportunities, or wonderful supportive parents. Those things are helpful but often not the case for most of us. Success is about how you respond to what life hands you. It's like the saying goes "if life hands you lemons, make lemonade." The point being if something seemingly bad happens to you, then make something good come of it. The women in this book certainly did that.

Have you ever heard anyone say that you should dress for success? What they meant was that you should dress the part, dress as if you already are who you want to be. An old manager of mine years ago told me that I should dress like the other managers until I became one. That's what I did, and even though I started at entry level, within two years I was an executive manager with my company. It wasn't new advice, people have been saying that for years. Jack Canfield adds to that another way; Jack is the author of the "Chicken Soup for the Soul" books; He says that you should also ACT AS IF.

ACT AS IF:

You have already attained your goals

You already are who you want to be

You feel successful, even if you don't yet feel that way

Every person you meet is on your side, and can help you succeed

It is impossible to fail

Personal Notes

_____

_____

_____

_____

_____

_____

_____

_____

_____

_____

_____

Virtual Book Tour

Tori plans on doing a physical book tour

at several locations around the country

And a virtual book tour

for those who can't travel to the physical locations

Visit Tori's personal website to get information on

Book tour dates,

Special contests, free giveaways,

And speaking events

http://torivigil.tripod.com/bio

Enter this Book Code

AFG32B

Chapter seven

Words from the wise

Throughout my life I have found some truly great quotes, poems, funny stuff and ideas, that came from many well known, and not so well known people. The following are my favorite quotes that have blessed my life.

Enlightenment and laughter are both a part of our spiritual journey!

SCRIPTURES

THE LORDS PRAYER:

Our Father, who art in heaven,

hallowed be thy name.

Thy Kingdom come, thy will be done,

on earth as it is in heaven

Give us this day our daily bread.

And forgive us our trespasses,

as we forgive those who trespass against us.

And lead us not into temptation,

but deliver us from evil.

For thine is the kingdom, the power and the glory. Forever and

ever. Amen

Phillipians 4:8

Whatsoever things are true

Whatsoever things are honest

Whatsoever things are just

Whatsoever things are pure

Whatsoever things are lovely

Whatsoever things are of good report

If there be any virtue and

If there be any praise

THINK ON THESE THINGS!

Matthew 22:37-38 "Love the Lord your God with all your heart and with all your soul, and with all your mind. This is the first and greatest commandment."

Psalm 5:12 says, "Favor surrounds the righteous like a shield."

Hebrews 11:1 "Now faith is the substance of things hoped for, and the evidence of things not seen."

Psalm 23:1-6 "The Lord is my shepherd I shall not want. He maketh me to lie down in green pastures: he leadeth me beside the still waters. He restoreth my soul. Yea, though I walk through the valley of the shadow of death, I will fear no evil: for thou art with me; thy rod and thy staff they comfort me. Thou prepares a table before me in the presence of mine enemies: thou anointest m]

y head with oil; my cup overflows. Surely goodness and mercy shall follow me all the days of my life: and I will dwell in the house of the Lord for ever."

Psalm 139:14 "I have been fearfully and wonderfully made"

Proverbs 11:24-25 "It is possible to give away and become richer. It is also possible to hold on too tightly and loose everything. Yes the liberal man shall be rich! By watering others, he waters himself."

1 Corinthians 13:4-7 "Love is very patient and kind, never jealous or envious, never boastful or proud, never haughty or selfish or rude. Love does not demand its own way. It is not irritable or touchy. It does not hold grudges and will hardly even no-

tice when others do it wrong. It is never glad about injustice and is glad whenever truth wins.

Romans 12:2 says "and be not conformed to this world: but be ye transformed by the renewing of your mind, that ye may prove what is that good, and acceptable, and perfect will of God."

2 TIMOTHY 1:6-7 "...stir into flame the strength and boldness that is in you...For the Holy Spirit, God's gift, does not want you to be afraid of people. But to be wise and strong and to love them and enjoy being with them. If you stir up this inner power you will never be afraid.

1 John 4:4 " you are from God, little children, and have over-come them; for greater is he who is in you than he who is in the world."

Isaiah 54:17   "No weapon formed against you shall prosper...This is the heritage of the servants of the Lord, and their righteousness is from Me, says the Lord."

Joel 2:28 "And afterward, I will pour out my Spirit on all people. Your sons and daughters will prophesy, your old men will dream dreams, your young men will see visions."

Hebrews 13:5 God said "I will never leave you; I will never abandon you."

QUOTES – AUTHOR UNKNOWN

"Pursue quality in your work first- money will follow"

"When you undervalue what you do, the world will undervalue who you are"

"Know thyself and thou shalt know all the mysteries of the gods and of the universe"

"Only one life will soon be past—only what's done for Christ will last."

If at first you don't succeed, then try, try again.

I sought my soul, but my soul I could not see.

I sought my God, but my God eluded me.

I sought my brother, and found all three........

Sow a thought, Reap an action;

Sow an action, Reap a habit;

Sow a habit, Reap a character;

Sow a character, Reap a destiny.

There is no light for those who don't know darkness

The will of God will never take you where the grace of God will

not protect you

In the light of Eternity, Does it really matter?

QUOTES IN ALPHABETICAL ORDER BY AUTHOR/SPEAKER

ANAIS NIN

We don't see things as they are, we see things as we are...

ARISTOTLE

Education is the best provision for the journey to old age.

We are what we repeatedly do; excellence then is not an act, but a habit.

Men acquire a particular quality by constantly acting a particular way

Acquire bravery by performing brave actions

Acquire justice by performing just actions

Acquire knowledge by acting in a knowledgeable way, seek knowledge.

and so on.....

ALBERT EINSTEIN

Great spirits have always encountered violent opposition from mediocre minds.

Imagination is more important than knowledge.

Try not to become a man of success but rather a man of value.

We cannot solve our problems with the same level of thinking that created them.

The state of mind which enables a man to do work of this kind...is akin to that of the religious worshiper or the lover: the daily effort comes from no deliberate intention or program, but straight from the heart.

I assert that the cosmic religious experience is the strongest and the noblest driving force...

ALBERT ELLIS

People and things do not upset us, rather we upset ourselves by believing they can upset us.

ANNE MORROW LINDBERGH

The most exhausting thing in life, I have discovered, is insincerity.

ABRAHAM LINCOLN

People are about as happy as they make up their minds to be...

Your own resolution to succeed is more important than any other one thing....

AMBROSE REDMOON

Courage is not the absence of fear, but rather the judgment that something else is more important than fear.

BOOKER T. WASHINGTON

I have learned that success is to be measured not so much by the position that one has reached in life as by the obstacles overcome while trying to succeed."

BARUCH SPINOZA

I saw that all things I feared, and which feared me, had nothing good or bad in them save in-so-far as the mind was affected by them...

Every existence has a universal or essential character, although to realize this character the existent thing must transcend its own intrinsic form, that is, free itself from the boundaries of its own structure.

BEVERLY SILLS

You may be disappointed if you fail, but you are doomed if you don't try.

BISHOP VERON ASHE

You can't be like Christ, until you SEE him as he really is.

CHARLES DICKENS

No man is useless who lightens the burdens of another.

DENIS WAITLEY

The truly successful person inspires others to do more than they have thought possible for themselves.

DWIGHT EISENHOWER

No one can defeat us unless we first defeat ourselves.

DR. MARTIN LUTHER KING JR.

I have a dream that one day this nation will rise up, live out the true meaning of its creed, "We hold these truths to be self-evident; that all men are created equal."

Take the first step of faith, you don't have to see the whole staircase.

DEEPAK CHOPRA

Beneath the layers of chaos and uncertainty something creative is always happening.

Success is the expansion of happiness

ELEANOR ROOSEVELT

No one can make you feel inferior without your consent.

You gain strength, courage and confidence in every experience in which you really stop to look fear in the face... you must do the thing you think you can not do.

EARNEST HEMMINGWAY

Courage is grace under pressure.

ECKHART TOLLE

You can not fight against ego and win, just as you can not fight against darkness. The light of consciousness is all that's necessary, and you are the light.

FACING THE GIANTS (movie)

Your actions will always follow your beliefs

FRANKLIN D. ROOSEVELT

The only thing we have to fear is fear itself.

Happiness lies not in the mere possession of money: it lies in the joy of achievement, in the thrill of creative effort.

Small wonder that confidence languishes, for it thrives only on honesty, on honor, on the sacredness of obligations, on faithful protection, on unselfish performance, without them it can not live.

GANDHI

Happiness is when what you think, what you say and what you do
are all in harmony

Be the change you want to see in the world

GOETHE

Things which matter most must never be at the mercy of things which matter least.

HENRY BLACKABY

How I live my life is a testimony of what I believe about God.

HERM ALBRIGHT

A positive attitude may not solve all your problems, but it will annoy enough people to make it worth the effort.

HELEN KELLER

Self-pity is our worst enemy and if we yield to it, we can never do anything wise in the world.

Faith is the strength by which a shattered world shall emerge into the light.

HENRY DAVID THOREAU

If one advances confidently in the direction of his dreams, and endeavors to live the life which he has imagined he will meet with a success unexpected in common hours

With a little more deliberation in the choice of their pursuits all men would perhaps become essentially students and observers, for certainly their nature and destiny are interesting to all alike.

There is no remedy for love but to love more...

Success usually comes to those who are too busy to be looking for it.

Do not hire a man who does your work for money. But him who does it for the love of it.

For every thousand hacking at the leaves of evil, there is one striking at the root.

JESUS

As you think, so shall you be..

JOE NUNZIATA

You must see yourself, and your individual contributions as meaningful to the world. When you place yourself in this elevated light it is impossible to minimize your value as a human being.

JOSHUA WOODEN

Don't try to be better than somebody else, but never cease trying to be the best you can be...

JOHN FISHER

John Fisher wrote: "A good man is not a perfect man; a good man is an honest man, faithful and unhesitatingly responsive to the voice of God in his life."

JOHN TESH

It's time to get passionate about your life, it's time to move your life from the place you are right now to the place you were meant to be.

JOHN WOODEN

There is a choice you have to make, in everything you do,

so keep in mind that in the end, the choice you make, makes

you...

Four things a man must learn to do if he would make his life

more true:

To think without confusion clearly,

To love his fellow man sincerely,

To act from honest motives purely,

To trust in God and Heaven securely.

JOHN GREENLEAF WHITTIER

For all the sad words of tongue or pen

The saddest are these: "It might have been".

JOHN D. ROCKEFELLER, JR.

I believe that every right implies a responsibility; every opportunity an obligation; every possession a duty.

JOHN BUNYAN

In prayer, it is better to have a heart without words than words without heart.

JFK

When power leads man towards arrogance, poetry reminds him of his limitations. When power narrows the area of man's concern, poetry reminds him of the richness and diversity of his existence. When power corrupts, poetry cleanses. For art establishes the basic human truth which must serve as the touchstone of our judgment.

KENT SAYRE

With Unstoppable Confidence, People Will Be Magnetically Drawn To You Because People Like People Who Believe In Themselves.

Become Aware That The Only Way To Fail Is To Quit Altogether And That You Learn From Each Mistake And Grow From It .

KIM CLEMENT

SEEK the kingdom

SEE the kingdom (that you sought)

ENTER the kingdom (that you saw)

INHERIT the kingdom (that you entered)

POSSESS the kingdom (that you inherited)

Shake the unshakeable

Break the unbreakable

Move the unmoveable

Touch the untouchable

Reach the unreachable

Defy the defiant

Prophecy to dead bone

Antagonize the devil

And go shout it on the mountain that Jesus Christ is Lord

LESS BROWN

Shoot for the moon, even if you miss you'll land among the
stars.

LONG FELLOW

Oh fear not in a world like this, and thou shall know erelong,
know

how sublime a thing to suffer and be strong.

MOTHER TERESA

I see Jesus Christ everyday in all of his distressing disguises.

Life is not worth living unless it is lived for others.

If you can't feed a hundred people then feed just one.

MICHEAL ANGELO

Every beauty that is seen here bellow by persons of perception

Resembles more than anything else the celestial source from which we all came.

The greater danger for most of us Is not that our aim is too high and we miss it, But that it is too low and we reach it.

MICHEAL JORDAN

I have missed more than 9000 shots in my career. I have lost almost 300 games. On 26 occasions I have been entrusted to take the game winning shot... and missed. And I have failed over and over and over again in my life. And that is why... I succeed.

MARGARET THATCHER

You may have to fight a battle more than once to win.

MORRIE SCHWARTZ

Forgive everybody everything....Accept the past as past, without denying it or discarding it. Reminisce about it, but don't live in it, Learn from it, but don't punish yourself about it or continually regret it. And don't get stuck in it......

Death ends a life not a relationship.......

keep your heart open for as long as you can, as wide as you can, for others and especially for yourself......
Be a witness to yourself. Act as an observer to your own physical, emotional, social, and spiritual states.....

MEISTER ECKHART

The eye, with which I see, God sees me; My eye and Gods eye are one eye, one seeing, one realizing, and one love.

MOTHER OF WAYNE DYER

A mother can but guide...then step aside

MAYA ANGELOU

I've learned that people will forget what you said, people will forget what you did, but people will never forget how you made them feel.

A woman's heart should be so hidden in Christ that a man should have to seek Him first to find her.

NELSON MANDELA

We are powerful beyond measure

NORMAN VINCENT

Change your thoughts and you change your world....

OPRAH WINDFREY

I act as if everything depends on me, and pray as if everything depends on GOD.

Don't complain about what you don't have. Use what you've got. To do less than your best is a sin.

I believe that you tend to create your own blessings. You

have to prepare yourself so that when opportunity comes, you're ready.

OLIVER WENDELL HOLMES

What lies behind us and what lies before us are tiny matters compared to what lies within us.

PEACEFUL WARRIOR (movie)

"There is never nothing going on"

"WHERE ARE YOU? right here, WHAT TIME IS IT?, now WHAT ARE YOU?, this moment"

"Our thoughts are not who we are"

"Find your answers from within"

"There is no starting or stopping only doing"

"There are no ordinary moments"

"Knowledge is knowing how to do something, Wisdom is doing it"

"Be conscience about your choices and responsible about your actions"

"The people that are the hardest to love are usually the ones who need it the most"

PATANJALI

When you are inspired by some great purpose, some extraordinary project, all your thoughts break their bonds; your mind transcends limitations, your consciousness expands in every direction, and you find yourself in a new, great and wonderful world. Dormant forces, faculties and talents become alive and you discover yourself to be a greater person by far than you ever dreamed yourself to be.

PRESIDENT HARRY S. TRUMAN

It is amazing what you can accomplish if you do not care who gets the credit."

PYTHAGORAS

Learn to be silent, let your quiet mind listen and absorb.

RUDYARD KIPLING

I kept six honest serving men. They taught me all I knew.

Their names are What and Why and When and How and

Where and Who

RALPH WALDO EMERSON

We become what we think about all day long...

Enthusiasm is the mother of effort, and without it nothing

great was ever accomplished.

RICHARD GREENE

To the magical creative force that, every once in a while,

shines through the thoughts, passions and words of mere

mortals, lifting them - and all of us - to experience the di-

vine."

ROBERT HALF

Persistence is what makes the impossible possible, the possi-

ble likely, the likely definite.

RICK WARREN

Your perspective will influence how you invest your time, spend your money, use your talents, and value your relationships..

How you define life determines your destiny

Fear is a self-imposed prison that will keep you from becoming what God intends for you to be.

Without a purpose life is motion without meaning, activity without direction, and events without a reason.

The greatest tragedy is not death, but a life without purpose...

SAMUEL JOHNSON

There can be no friendship without confidence and no confidence without integrity.

SOCRATES

The individual must experience life directly and not depend on logic or borrowed learning. The aim is to achieve union with ultimate love. By knowing the beauty of the body, the beauty of the soul, and at last the impersonal beauty of the universe pulsating inside and outside the silent being.

The really important thing is not to live, but to live well.

SHAKESPEARE

There is nothing either good or bad, but thinking makes it so...

Cowards die many times before their deaths. The valiant never taste of death but once.

SAINT AUGUSTINE

Thou shall love they neighbor as thyself, but thou shall love God with all thy heart, and with all thy soul and with all thy mind....For when He says, "with all thy heart, and with all thy soul, and with all thy mind", He means that no part of our life is to be unoccupied, and to afford room for the wish to enjoy some other object, but whatever else may suggest itself to us as an object worthy of love is to borne into the same channel in which the whole current of our affection flows. Whoever then, loves his neighbor aright, ought to urge upon him that he too should love God with his whole heart and soul and mind. For in this way, loving his neighbor as himself, a man turns the whole current of his love both for himself and for his neighbor into the channel of the love of God....

STEVEN COVEY

Begin with the end in mind.

THOMAS EDISON

Opportunity is missed because it is dressed in overalls and looks like work.

Genius is one percent inspiration and ninety-nine percent perspiration.

T.D. JAKES

we can love others with no more wholeness than that which we love ourselves.....

It is the duty of every man to help his lady achieve her greatness....

You actually train others how to treat you by how you treat yourself....

Woman is a precious commodity. Through her all greatness is born. She is the mother of nations, the womb of creativity, the garden of life....

THEODORE ROOSEVELT

Now you see that if you think you can, or somebody who believes in you thinks you can, then you can.

"It is not the critic who counts; not the man who points out how the strong man stumbles, or where the doer of deeds could have done them better. The credit belongs to the man who is actually in the arena, whose face is marred by dust and sweat and blood, who strives valiantly;... but who does actually strive to do the deed; who knows the great enthusiasm, the great devotion, who spends himself in a worthy cause, who at the best knows in the end the triumph of high achievement and who at the worst, if he fails, at least he fails while daring greatly. So that his place shall never be with those cold and timid souls who know neither victory nor defeat."

TENNYSON

Tis better to have loved and lost than never to have loved at all.

VOLTAIRE

Judge a man by his questions, rather than by his answers!

WALLACE D. WATTLES

It is the desire of God that you should get rich. He wants you to get rich because he can express himself better through you if you have plenty of things to use in giving him expression. He can live more in you if you have unlimited command of the means of life.

WAYNE W. DYER

Circumstances do not make me who I am, they simply reveal who I have chosen to be....

It is not what is in the world that determines the quality of your life, it is how you choose to process your world in your thoughts....

Don't die with your music still in you!...

When you judge another person, you do not define him or her, you define yourself....

I like to think of God as the ocean and myself as a glass. If I dip the glass into the ocean, I will have a glass full of God. No matter how I analyze this, it will still contain God. Now, the glass of God is not as big as the ocean nor is it omniscient or omnipotent, but it is still God.

Prayer is you talking to God, Intuition is God talking to you.......

Within you lies a divine capacity to manifest or attract all you need or desire

Circumstances do not make me who I am, they simply reveal who I have chosen to be...

WINSTON CHURCHILL

Never give in, never, never - in nothing, great or small, large or petty -never give in except to convictions of honor and good sense. Never yield to force; never yield to the apparently overwhelming might of the enemy.

You create your own universe as you go along.

WILLIAM JAMES

Human beings, by changing the inner attitudes of their minds, can change the outer aspects of their lives. It is our consistent actions (our habits) which more than anything else determine the direction and success of our lives. Thus, the first key to success is to adopt good habits.

An ounce of prevention is worth a pound of cure...

In serving one another we become free...

Don't just watch but see, Don't just hear but listen, Don't just talk but communicate...

No written word, nor spoken plea can teach our youth what

they should be. Nor all the books on all the shelves, It's what the teachers are themselves...

Discipline yourself and others won't have to...

Talent is God given; be humble.

Fame is man given; be thankful.

Conceit is self given; be careful.

I'm not what I ought to be, Not what I want to be, Not what I'm going to be but I am thankful that I'm better than I used to be...

For when the ONE GREAT SCORER comes to write against your name, He writes not that you won or lost, but how you played the game...

POETRY

BY TORI VIGIL

There are two types of people in society today.

There are those who say the nature of humanity is cruel

They focus on what's wrong and see no change in site.

There are those who say humanity is capable of great things

They focus on what's right and good and try to do the same.

There are two types of people with vastly differing views;

Of these two types of people which one, my friend are you.

SAINT FRANCIS OF ASSISI

Lord, make me an instrument of your peace.

Where there is hatred let me sow love,

where there is injury pardon,

Where there is doubt, faith,

Where there is despair, hope,

Where there is darkness, light,

And where there is sadness, joy

Oh diving master grant that I may

Not so much seek to be consoled as to console;

To be understood as to understand;

To be loved as to love;

For it is in giving that we receive;

It is in pardoning that we are pardoned;

And it is in dying that we are born to eternal life.

Letting Go, Author Unknown

To let go doesn't mean to stop caring; it means that I can't do it for someone else. To let go is not to cut myself off; it is the realization that I can't control another. To let go is not to enable, it is to allow learning from natural consequences. To let go is to admit powerlessness, which means that the outcome is not in my hands. To let go is not to try to change or blame another, it is that I can only change myself. To let go is not to fix, it is to be supportive. To let go is not to be in the middle arranging all the outcomes; it is to allow others to effect their own outcomes. To let go is not to be protective; it is to permit another to face reality. To let go is not to deny, it is to accept. To let go is not to nag, scold, or to argue, it is to search my own shortcomings and correct them. To let go is not to adjust everything to my desires; it is to take each day as it comes and to cherish the moment. To let go is not to regret the past, and is to grow in the present. To let go is to fear less and love more.

The optimists Creed

I Promise myself :

To be so strong that nothing can disturb my peace of mind.
To talk health, happiness, and prosperity to every person I meet.
To make all my friends feel that there is something worthwhile in them. To look at the sunny side of everything and make my optimism come true. To think only of the best, to work only for

the best and to expect only the best. To be just as enthusiastic about the success of others as I am about my own. To forget the mistakes of the past and press on to the greater achievements of the future.

To wear a cheerful expression at all times and give a smile to every living creature I meet. To give so much time to improving myself that I have no time to criticize others. To be too large for worry, too noble for anger, too strong for fear, and too happy to permit the presence of trouble. To think well of myself and to proclaim this fact to the world, not in loud word, but in great deeds. To live in the faith that the whole world is on my side, so long as I am true to the best that is in me.

Ten other Outstanding Women in history you should get to know

Pocahontas (helped the pilgrims and saved John Smith)

Sacagawea (Native American who helped Lewis and Clark)

Susan B. Anthony (pioneer in the fight for women's rights)

By Tori Vigil

Helen Keller (blind writer)

Amelia Earhart (female pilot)

Bessie Coleman (African American Stunt pilot)

Georgia O'Keeffe (painter)

Willma P. Mankiller (first female tribal Chief)

Ruth Handler (creator of Barbie)

Oprah Winfrey (chairman of Harpo inc.)

Personal Notes

Chapter Eight

The Gift of Philanthropy

"Charity is a supreme virtue, and the great channel through which the mercy of God is passed on to mankind. It is the virtue that unites men and inspires their noblest efforts."

-Conrad Hilton-

Mother Teresa once said "it is not the magnitude of our actions, but the amount of love that is put into them that matters; it is in the path of service to others that we come to know Christ". Service to others in any form, large or small is the expression of the love you hold in your heart. We are only pencils in the hand of the most gifted writer, paintbrushes in the hand of the divine painter; and instruments in the hands of the great musician, GOD. Our service is the means by which God touches the world.

If you look in the dictionary you will see philanthropy described as "the effort or inclination to increase the well-being of humankind." What could increase mankind's well-being more than expanding love. With every act of kindness, generosity, or the giving of a gift there is a measure of love involved. This kind of love is often referred to as Agape Love; Agape is the Greek word meaning "Pure love, to love another for their sake." Agape love gives with no thought of reward, any demand, or expectation of reciprocation. In this type of giving, love becomes more than a word, more than an emotion, love becomes a choice. We can choose to show God's Agape love to others through the giving of our gifts, talents, abilities, money, and time.

The women in this book strongly believe in the organizations that give back, and help elevate humanity to higher levels of consciousness, and deeper levels of spirituality. We encourage every woman to get involved in their own community whether as a staff member, leader, or volunteer with a philanthropic organization, a school, or just a worthy cause. When you give of yourself often you will find you get more in return than what you give. The joys and rewards that can be found in philanthropic activities are many and varied. It's easy to give money we can all do that even if it's just a few cents here and there; it's not so easy to give your time, talents, gifts, and abilities.

"Let us not be satisfied with just giving money. Money is not enough, money can be got, but they need your hearts to love them. So, spread your love everywhere you go." -Mother Teresa-

So many times I've heard women say that they just don't have anything to offer a non-profit organization, especially if they are a stay at home mom. Every woman has skills, perhaps a hobby, or something that interests them. Find a way to use that skill, pursue that hobby, or interest in a way that benefits others. A woman in our church loves to knit, so every time a new baby is born to one of our church members, she knits them a baby blanket. Having received 2 such blankets at the birth of my twins, I can tell you it touches deep into a mother's heart, and later deep into the heart of that child. My own mother loves to spend time with the elderly, my sister loves to be around children, and I love to write. There are countless organizations out there that are in need of someone who can do what you love to do.

Even if you can't give of your time you can still give of your talents. Non-profits are always seeking items to give to the needy, or to use in auctions which help them raise funds for their organization. Find a way to spread love, and you will reap more love in return.

"Before volunteering for anything, we should consider our priorities. If we know we can volunteer our time without neglecting our relationship with GOD, or our relationship with spouse and family, then we can try to determine exactly how much time we can devote to the cause. Or if a family member will volunteer with us, we can have time with them while we further the cause" -Susan Wolf-

Today we may find ourselves in the position to be able to help another, but tomorrow we may find ourselves on the receiving end of help from others. My family and I found ourselves in that situation when we lived in Florida, there was a huge hurricane evacuation. Everyone was fleeing the state driving west on interstate 10. The roads were littered with cars as traffic came to a complete stop, and we found ourselves in Georgia. There were no hotel rooms, no standing room in hotel lobbies, and the only place we found shelter was at a Red Cross camp. The people there fed us; they gave us beds and blankets; and medicine for our daughter who in the stress of everything had gotten a very high fever. We can't thank those volunteers enough for being there for us with their kindness, and understanding when we needed them most. Philanthropy is much more than filling a need, volunteering your time, or raising funds. It's about making life better for all humanity. That kind of impact usually happens by touching the life of one person at a time.

"It is easy to love the people far away. It is not always easy to love those close to us. It is easier to give a cup of rice to relieve hunger than to relieve the loneliness and pain of someone unloved in our own home. Bring love into your home for this is where our love for each other must start."-Mother Teresa-

One of the things I love most about Mother Teresa is the fact that she doesn't just encourage people to give, but to give out of love. Love is a positive and affirming emotion, Love is a state of being, Love is energy, and Love vibrates on the highest frequency. Philanthropy can not solve all the problems of the world, but if it helps spread love, then it can solve the cause of most problems; hatred, which of course is the lack of love. Often the hardest people to love are usually the ones who need it the most. Hatred is contagious so don't allow yourself to be infected, choose instead to eradicate hatred with love. Mother Teresa once said she would never attend a rally against war, but she would attend a rally for peace. Hating war only generates more hate because the focus is on the negative emotion of hate; instead focus on the positive, on love and peace then seek after it. It is the same for any situation, circumstance, or person in your life right now. You can not fight fire with fire; to put out the fire you need it's opposite, water.

"If I give everything I have to feed the poor, and hand over my body to be burned but have not love, I gain nothing…

Love is patient; love is kind. Love is not jealous, it does not put on airs, and it is not snobbish. Love is never rude, it is not self-seeking, it is not prone to anger; neither does it brood over injuries. Love does not rejoice in what is wrong but rejoices with the truth. There is no limit to love's forbearance, to its trust, its hope, its power to endure. Love never fails." –The Bible, the book of Corinthians-

The following is a small list of the organizations the ladies in this book have worked with, or support, feel free to email info about the one's you have found perhaps if this book is every expanded in a second edition I can add them.

TEEN ORGANIZATIONS

- The Angel to Angel Network   (reaching out to Native American Teens)

  www.angeltoangelnetwork.com

- Boys and Girls Clubs of America www.bgca.org

- Writers in Schools WITS (encouraging kids to read and write, a Texas program) www.witshouston.org

- Arts Street (helping inner city kids make a living at being creative, a Colorado program) www.arts-street.org

- Acquire The Fire (teen conferences around the country) www.acquirethefire.com

NON PROFIT MINISTRIES

- Kingdom Works International (educates & equips Christians and pastors for ministry)   228-769-7510

  - www.kingdom-works.org

- Kim Clement (Prophetic Image Expressions, equipping the new generation of prophets) www.kimclement.com

- Gulf Coast Association of Christian Entertainers and Filmmakers www.mooviemakers4GOD.com Mission statement: to offer the Christian community good, clean, wholesome entertainment and to produce films that teach evangelism concepts and godly truths.

- To women with love www.towomenwithlove.info

CRISIS ORGANIZATIONS

- Care-Net Crisis Pregnancy Centers

  www.care-net.com

- S.O.A.R. (Speaking Out About Rape)

  www.soar.com

- Our Daily Bread (feeds the homeless of Pascagoula, MS)

  228-769-7515

- Child Advocates of Fort Bend (providing a voice for abused children)   www.cafb.org

- A.H.H.S. (A helping hand for healing souls, helps raise awareness about child abuse and helps survivors of child abuse)   http://warriorwomyn31.tripod.com

CONTACT INFORMATION:

Contact Tori

http://torivigil.tripod.com

Contact J'Lynn

www.newvirtuepageants.com

www.towomenwithlove.info

Contact Brandie

ImageArtistry@Earthlink.net

Contact Susan

www.mooviemakers4GOD.com

Also from Tori Vigil

 Surviving the Teenage Journey, published 2006. Tori's first published book provides guidance and information to help teens make good life choices, and discover their inner voice. Written for both teens and their care givers, author Tori Vigil shares her personal story as a teenage parent, as well as letters from women, and girls who have dealt with difficult situations in their own lives, to encourage and support the decision making skills of teen girls.

 Angels of Mercy greeting card collection... Show God's mercy and touch someone's heart today with a Tori Vigil greeting card from the Angel of Mercy collection.

 Matted prints by Tori Vigil... Express your heart, and touch someone's life with the gift of a Tori Vigil matted print. It's a gift they'll never forget that can be framed and displayed in their home or office.

By Tori Vigil

Made in the USA

www.ingramcontent.com/pod-product-compliance
Lightning Source LLC
Chambersburg PA
CBHW062140280526
45788CB00001B/232